AF255201

Mentioning the Unmentionables

Mentioning the Unmentionables

Naming the Corrosive Threat to Our Lives Together and
Our Faithful Response in the Body of Christ

CHRIS HEATON

WIPF & STOCK · Eugene, Oregon

MENTIONING THE UNMENTIONABLES
Naming the Corrosive Threat to Our Lives Together and Our Faithful Response in
the Body of Christ

Wipf & Stock
An Imprint of Wipf and Stock Publishers
199 W. 8th Ave., Suite 3
Eugene, OR 97401

www.wipfandstock.com

PAPERBACK ISBN: 978-1-6667-8970-6
HARDCOVER ISBN: 978-1-6667-8971-3
EBOOK ISBN: 978-1-6667-8972-0

VERSION NUMBER 11/16/23

To my wife Abigail . . . who has always been patient with,
encouraging to, and prayerful for her husband.

Finally, then, brothers, we ask and urge you in the Lord Jesus, that as you received from us how you ought to walk and to please God, just as you are doing, that you do so more and more. For you know what instructions we gave you through the Lord Jesus. For this is the will of God, your sanctification: that you abstain from sexual immorality; that each one of you know how to control his own body in holiness and honor, not in the passion of lust like the Gentiles who do not know God; that no one transgress and wrong his brother in this matter, because the Lord is an avenger in all these things, as we told you beforehand and solemnly warned you. For God has not called us for impurity, but in holiness. Therefore whoever disregards this, disregards not man but God, who gives his Holy Spirit to you.

—1 Thess 4:1–8

Contents

Contents

Introduction
A First Conversation

WHAT WE HAVE BEEN doing is not working.

I had an inkling that something was "missing" in our conversations within the church. As I became more active in worship in my twenties, and more active in Bible study in my thirties, the world of the Scriptures began to form and shape more of who I was. But it was with a "reading project" in 2011–12 that things really changed. Starting in August, I read a letter of St. Paul every day for a year. *And it changed my life.* Not all of a sudden, but in a quiet, shuffling way. Quiet but *profound.* Because I was exposed to Paul, *all of him,* in a way I never had been before. I started to view the universe differently. In weekly worship you get *bits* of Paul (and the rest of the Bible), but my reading project revealed the other parts too. And I was changed for the better.

Then I started to explore some of the themes I found in the "secret parts" of Paul. I began looking for resources that talked about men and women, about marriage, about life together in a society that is hostile to God's truth. And *sexual morality.* The things that were increasingly on my mind as a Christian husband and father. Because what I saw all around me didn't square with what I knew of Christ and what Paul proclaimed in his letters. That's when I "discovered" Joel Biermann, professor of systematic theology at Concordia Seminary, St. Louis. Searching for resources on the seminary's website, I found a Lay Bible Institute entitled "Man and Woman According to God's Plan" taught by Dr. Biermann. Four sessions, two parts each, eight hours total. I was changed, or should I say "formed" again . . . for the better.

For here was someone in my denomination[1] *finally mentioning* things that had been on my mind, that had bothered me, that I knew I failed in . . . and that Paul discussed. I was a father and husband, but not a very good one. An accidental sort. But Dr. Biermann taught about God's *purpose* for man and woman within the world, within marriage. There is an order, an arrangement to all of it, and *it's tied to God's good creation*. Marriage, it seems, is modeled after Jesus and his bride, the church. What I read in Paul and learned from Dr. Biermann coalesced into a beautiful picture, but also a picture of something I was missing. Something I didn't see in my work, in the world, and often in the congregations at large.

So, in 2014, I went to the seminary. Concordia St. Louis. I was forty-two years old. For four years I was formed and shaped. I was trained and taught. I had exposure to some of the best minds and practitioners in the LCMS. I was intentionally prepared. I was ready to go out into the ministry and deliver the gospel! However, when I received my call to a congregation, and got started in ministry, I then learned how truly broken and sinful our families are, our marriages are, our people are. Not because the people of my congregation were better or worse . . . *they were typical of what you find everywhere, all throughout the church of God, all throughout the United States*. So, the question became: *What difference could I make?*

I have two daughters. During this journey and growth I also began to think more and more deeply about the men I wanted them to someday marry. About my future sons-in-law and who I hoped they would be. About the world I wanted them and their children to live in and raise their families. To be sure, we as Christians look at things with an eternal perspective. *But God's world and our life together matter.* This is a scary place and getting scarier by the second. But something slowly dawned on me. While people were constantly "up in arms" about this thing or that, the next week it would be something else. I myself couldn't remember what my wife and I were so passionately discussing over dinner from one week to the next! *But what about the root causes?* We scream about the symptoms, but what about the things that give them growth? The places they come from? So, I started doing some work. Reading, listening, praying, observing, writing, consulting.

In June of 2022, I went to my district's pastor's convention. It was outstanding. Much was discussed. Many "elephants in the room" were addressed. LCMS President Matthew Harrison gave a terrific presentation. I

---

1. My denomination being The Lutheran Church—Missouri Synod, a confessional denomination of the Evangelical Lutheran Church. Hereafter referred to as the LCMS.

felt very positive about the direction we were headed as a synod. A lot of things got mentioned . . . but one thing was *noticeably absent*. Something that in my work on root causes I knew to be *a major problem not just in the world, but in the church*. But there was nothing but silence. No one said a word about it. Like it didn't exist and wasn't an issue. *But I knew it to be the biggest problem facing all of us*. An existential threat to our society and congregational life together. *Pornography*. I was compelled to say something.

So I decided to write this book.

Full disclosure—I'm not a writer. I mean, I write . . . but I am not a *trained* writer. After reading this you may agree! But I have a lot to say. Perhaps too much. This book is not principally data driven. There are myriads of books on the market citing study after study regarding my topic. This is not a book that is challenging "the culture" to some great awakening. This book is written *to Christians*. My target and imagined audience is *concerned lay people from the Lutheran tradition (though not exclusively), who are troubled and even frightened about what they see in the world today and seek a response*. This book is for the sinner trapped in the habitual sin of pornography who wants to stop. This book is for the parents who want something to guide and encourage their raising of faithful Christian children and protect them from pornography. This book is for those in the church who want a response to what has seeped into our fellowship. This book relies heavily on my experiences, my failures, and then what I've learned, both as a fifty-two-year-old man as well as a pastor. More than just calling out what's wrong, this book is also about what our faithful response should be if we take God's word and his good design and order seriously.

You may encounter some surprising topics—teaching the faith and pedagogy, dating, Billy Joel, yoga pants, confessional and faithful worship—but many of these things are a *part of the tapestry of both what we face and how we are to respond*. This book is written to be read in order, but could be read topically, jumping around as it suits the reader. I realize people lead busy lives and want something for the moment, intending to come back later. This book works that way too.

Some of you from faithful Christian traditions may be looking for primarily a "gospel response." To be sure, the gospel of Jesus Christ—the forgiveness of sins in him alone—runs through this book like a thread. It is centered on his grace and mercy. But our topic also requires a response of God's word of law. You may at times feel as if there is an over-emphasis on the law and "what we do." This is by design. For we rightly divide and distinguish the work of the law from the work of the gospel. God's word is both. So, we listen to what God's truth tells us with a tension—*we can do nothing to save ourselves*, and in fact, any act of holiness is predicated on the work of the Holy Spirit alone. Yet we are called to live faithful lives and seek out faithful, practical solutions to the threats we face (*so, our effort is required*). This is in keeping with the revelation of Holy Scripture.[2]

I hope you find this Christ-centered work edifying and enlightening. If nothing else, I hope this starts some conversations in your corner of the world. May God be praised!

Reformation Day, 2023

---

2. For a terrific exposition of this duality, see Biermann, *Case for Character*.

PART ONE

Disclosing the Evil among Us

Chapter One

Mentioning the Unmentionables

In ages past, society employed a euphemism, prominent in the Victorian Age, known as "the unmentionables." The unmentionables could refer to any number of things (body parts, types of clothing, or behavior) and it was handy because it alluded to certain topics *without overtly mentioning them*. It protected people from saying or drawing attention to things that should not be said. Satan does great damage by tempting people to take the illicit and *putting it out in the open*. While not eliminating the illicit, the euphemism of "unmentionable" helped people keep those things from being on display and to be, well, titillating. Raising untoward curiosity. However, now it seems everything is on the table. The illicit is the explicit; our society has no unmentionables at all. We talk about any subject without compunction or restraint. We like to "keep it real" and "tell it like it is." What was once never discussed is now openly talked about with toddlers, bandied about among retirees, debated by teens with parents, dissected in print or online, delved into on Reddit or Instagram. *Depravity on full display*. We've lost this helpful euphemism of the unmentionables. But we've also lost so much more.

As a society, we've lost any ability to discern between good and evil. There are no longer agreed upon conventions of what is true and beautiful. There are no standards of behavior. *Everyone does what is right in his own eyes.* Every person, it seems, has their own definition of what is true *for them*, or "what works." Utilitarianism has replaced objective truth. The radical project of the progressive left seeks to undermine what is objectively good and replace it with perversions. Unmoored from biological sex and free to choose their own pronouns (or not), people feel empowered to determine a reality for themselves. Radical individualism rules the day. Life is a "choose your own adventure story." Pilate's aphorism "What is truth?" is the starting point, and "my truth" the relative outcome.

We've also lost our ability (and desire) to reason and debate. To consider and respond. To listen and ponder . . . then offer a rebuttal (if that's needed) or a kind word (if that's what is required). The topics of the day are just "out there." The result is chaos and a continual state of outrage. People are confronted with every conceivable situation in an age where few have the character and courage to address the obvious issues of the day and at the same time navigate what should *not* be said. The topics *du jour* are discussed in a way that rarely gets to the heart of the matter without mentioning every single thing in every single situation. So, we live in a paradox. *Saying everything and saying nothing at the same time.* While people have no filters, irrespective of audience, yet at the same time we struggle to openly and winsomely engage in *root causes of the ills of society* . . . and where needed, to pull up the roots.

This is a "we" problem—including those of us in the church. As stated in the introduction, I write to Christians. We too imbibe deeply in a culture that is corrosive, base, and ugly. This corrosion has seeped into our congregational lives like bad water into a leaky foundation. The response of many Christians is to drift through life, engage in everything that's out there and occasionally go to worship when it suits them. This creates a sinful tension—*living unrepentantly in ways that were once forbidden and clearly go against the teaching of the church* and *then demanding forgiveness for what ails them.* One way of handling this tension among Christians is to attempt to sanitize the unmentionables. Bring them in, empty them of anything *too* unseemly, and stick a Jesus label on them. *Voilà!* Now we're inclusive and still Christian! But all that has done is to bring wickedness into the church and cheapen her proclamation.

Another way to deal with the tension is *to get rid of sin.* There's hardly any behavior, life-style, or activity that is uniformly deemed sinful by many church-going people. The list is long—fornication, co-habitating, same-sex activity, watching *any* online content, immorality of any kind. We rationalize away the sin. This blurring of lines and lack of discernment shows us the nature of sin—it blinds the eyes and corrupts the heart. Sin is accepted instead of dealt with in confession and absolution. To sin is to transgress a boundary that God establishes. But what if we keep moving the boundaries or just out-and-out erase them? What is it, then, to be sinful or *actually be a sinner*? With fewer and fewer things considered a sin, *what are congregations confessing to God and one another on Sunday morning?* With so many unmentionables now mentioned, so much behavior normalized, are we even able to call a sin a sin anymore?

While addressing societal ills that are fully present in the church, I don't seek to solve the world's problems or cure the evils of this present darkness. Jesus Christ is over all and in all and through all. His Spirit is living and active and the Creator is in control. Christ's church is unassailable. *What I seek to do is shed light on troublesome topics and suggest several responses.* Writing within a Christian context and from a Lutheran confessional posture, my goal is to illuminate in order that we might be more discerning and faithful. I seek to address the threats we face and offer some practical solutions. *It's time we call sin a sin again.* To do this, I present a "triptych."[1] Part 1 diagnoses our current cultural situation[2] in order to, in a phrase, "call a thing what it is." Next, part 2 offers a biblical response, particularly from St. Paul, applying the sword of the Spirit to the people of God in every stage of life. Again, *I am writing to Christians.* I therefore appeal to God's word, truth, and will for his creation. If you are one looking for help with pornography personally, or trying to help someone overcome engagement with it, part 3 is for you. But this section goes beyond the individual and looks as well to practices in the family and church. My lasting aim is to suggest very practical (and mostly ancient) approaches that help us get nearer to what God envisions for our lives together, as we await our Lord's return to restore his creation in the resurrection to come.

I therefore will *mention the unmentionables*—focusing on one particular issue and related topics that have been in many places overlooked in the modern era of the church and the congregations of the body of Christ.

---

1. A triptych is a three-paneled work of art that is hinged together. Each panel displays a particular focus, while forming a completed whole.

2. For the purposes of our conversation, when I refer to "culture" I am speaking of *the prevailing thoughts and practices that have captured the imaginations of a majority of people.* These thoughts and practices are manifested in music, cinema, social platform dialogue, literature, etc.

Chapter Two

Pornography and a *PIL* Conversation

We start by naming the "unmentionable" subject. *Pornography*. It is a corrosive threat to our lives together, not only in society at large but inside the church. That's quite a statement. It sounds inflammatory, like it should be under a "Fox News Alert" banner. So, what do I mean? Well . . . pornography is everywhere. Directly or indirectly, it is a normal part of most people's lives. It has changed the way men and women relate, date, and marry. It has destroyed marriages. Pornography has helped remove the act of sex from monogamy within marriage, while reconstituting our society's ideas about sex. It has corrupted the very good biological identity that God gives. It has glorified lust. It has rewired our brains. It has made people more aggressive, rabidly immodest, and even violent. It is a threat to our youngest of sons and daughters. It is a co-conspirator and driver of the sex trafficking industry. Need I go on?

We've stopped trying to categorize, recognize, or even name it. *But we've also stopped talking about it as a danger.* As a threat. As a sin to be confessed. Don't misunderstand me . . . most any Christian would admit that "porn" is wrong. But that's usually as far as it goes. However, the statistics are damning (see chapter 3)—many Christians are viewing pornography on *a weekly basis.* However, except in some very specialized circles, it is never discussed even *in the church.* Almost like it doesn't exist. For those of you who attend Christian conferences or seminars, I challenge you to find the topic of pornography on the docket at any one of them.[1] I wonder why this is? I have theories, but I'd rather get on with calling it out in a full and direct way, that people might be moved to repentance and turn to Christ for forgiveness, to then respond by strengthening our lives of worship, family, and the study of God's word. In other words, discipleship.

However, this is tricky. By mentioning a topic like this overtly, one can titillate without intention by discussing some of the sordid details. Pornography is tricky for pastors to preach on (not that anyone is trying) because there are always little ears or "innocent hearts" who haven't yet been exposed. Do you risk bringing up something that might raise a curiosity? How specific should you be when seemingly everyone knows about everything? So, in the spirit of keeping some subject matters from being overtly mentioned, and in an effort to expand the discussion beyond a narrow focus, I address the difficult topic of pornography by using the acronym *PIL*.

- *P* stands for the Greek word *porneia* (pronounced por-nai-ah) which means "fornication, unchastity, sexual immorality." It also is the etymological root word for, well, you know.

- *I* stands for general *immorality*, not only of a sexual nature, but *an overall rejection of God's will* and an acceptance of practices that are wicked, base, and ugly.

- *L* stands for *licentiousness*, a state of "anything goes" or a "free to do whatever I want."

Therefore, this book is about more than a single topic, but a collection of interrelated ones, behaviors manifested in multiple ways that threaten us and undermine our relationships. The goal at the outset is to own the fact of the pervasiveness of pornography and the myriad of ways we have been affected. The acronym *PIL* seeks to mention the unmentionables, but also broadens the topic beyond that of just pornography.

Allow me to say a bit more about each component of *PIL*.

P—PORNEIA

Porneia[2] is *any kind of perversion of a sexual nature*. For example, St. Paul in 1 Cor 5:1 says, "It is actually reported that there is sexual immorality among

---

1. To be fair, this is based on my experience as an LCMS pastor.

2. There are several derivatives used for this word, but they come from the same root

you, and of a kind that is not tolerated even among pagans, for a man has his father's wife." In this case, Paul is speaking of an incident involving a member of the church at Corinth and his stepmother. This verse gets a fuller treatment in chapter 9. Note that Paul does not give graphic details, in part because his hearers know the offense, but also because it need not be salaciously discussed. While *we* may be fascinated with the sordid specifics, Paul leaves the particulars unsaid. What he does do is *condemn the behavior and exhort that the congregation deal with it in the strongest way possible*—both for the congregation's and offender's sakes. Note too that Paul is not delineating certain activities as acceptable and others as out-of-bounds. This is our modern approach to sexuality outside of marriage. We turn them into "case studies" to debate what is "permissible" and what "crosses a line." Paul does not engage in such casuistry. He says there is "sexual immorality among you." In other words, it's a problem to be dealt with now! *Porneia* is itself a general category that denotes *anything* that perverts or undermines God's intended use of good and fitting sexual intimacy between a husband and wife. We would do well to follow Paul's lead. Name it broadly, don't get stuck in graphic details, and deal with it in contrition and faith.

I—GENERAL IMMORALITY

Perhaps your inclination is, "This doesn't pertain to me. I don't engage in such behaviors!" Fair enough. Maybe sexual immorality is not your *particular* besetting sin. Though lust is a constant threat to the body of Christ and almost every living person, perhaps you are in a season of life where it's not a daily struggle.[3] But we must see that sins of a sexual nature fall within an even broader sphere of general immorality—*that which goes against God's design for his creation.*[4] Consider Rom 1:18: "For the wrath of God is revealed from heaven against all ungodliness and unrighteousness of men, who by their unrighteousness suppress the truth." Paul goes on to name homosexuality as enunciating the core issue—*the creature of God worships not the Creator but other creatures.* All sin rightly understood is a breaking of the First Commandment and is idolatry and rebellion. But Paul doesn't stop with that singular sin. He instead lists a whole hosts of sins, many of which have nothing

and denote the same range of activity.

3. Full-blown sarcasm here. Come to expect it.

4. This is broadly speaking the Law of God. I will refer to this throughout by capitalizing Law for emphasis.

to do *directly* with sexual perversion. The point is that sexual sins are connected to the sinful condition of man and his desire to worship himself and other things around him. We must see the issue of pornography as being situated in the fallen creation, and as rebellion against God.

The category of general *i*mmorality also serves to connect all of us to a myriad of issues. Widespread acceptance of pornography affects us all, first because sexual sins impact many people (not just offender and victim), but also because in our own ways, we all "put up with it readily enough."[5] While perhaps not engaging ourselves, there are many ways we overlook, go along with, laugh at, wink and give a knowing nod to the general acceptance of a multitude of gross immorality, including the use and acceptance of pornography. I give a real life example. Think of how many times you're driving down the interstate. Maybe you have the kids in the car, or you're with your spouse. You come upon billboard after billboard for "gentleman's clubs" or "adult stores." What is your reaction? Do you blush? Do you tell the children to avert their eyes from evil? *Or does it even register with you?* My guess is it's the third thing. We yawn. We shrug. "What can you do?" We don't think a thing about it. And that is the point.

L—LICENTIOUSNESS

Which leads to the third component of our triadic acronym, *l*icentiousness. Not a word that comes tripping off our cultural or congregational tongue! We might think of licentiousness as "a free-for-all" or having "license" to do whatever we want, whenever we want. This is especially prevalent with hedonists, those who *worship* pleasure and decadence. But all sinners (so you and me) love to use license to argue for *a lifestyle free of constraint, because self-governing humans want to have the freedom to choose to do whatever they please.* Licentiousness ensnares many in the church, ones who have been redeemed by Christ but fancy themselves "free" (they suppose) to engage in any activity. But consider Rom 6:20–23.

> For when you were slaves of sin, you were free in regard to righteousness. But what fruit were you getting at that time from the things of which you are now ashamed? For the end of those things is death. But now that you have been set free from sin and have become slaves of God, the fruit you get leads to sanctification and

5. 2 Cor 11:4.

> its end, eternal life. For the wages of sin is death, but the free gift of
> God is eternal life in Christ Jesus our Lord.

Although free from sin by the blood of Christ, we are *not* free in the gospel to keep sinning to get more grace. Paul's picture is one of *servitude*, either to God and the fruits of righteousness worked in us, or to a life of sin. Paul speaks of two options. Your chariot is pulled by either one of two horses. Only one can be the master of our lives. But sadly, the response of many Christians is to ignore God's desire, resist the Spirit, and openly engage in a variety of activities in the name of "freedom." *Given a gift, people turn that gift into a rationalization to keep sinning more and more.* We are susceptible to this perversion of freedom, especially in the Lutheran tradition! The good and right emphasis on the gospel, the free forgiveness of sins in Christ alone, leaves many feeling that we can "continue in sin that grace may abound."[6] The rationalization of *licentiousness* is a powerful weapon in the enemy's toolbox. It's the voice that whispers, "It's okay, Jesus loves you! Keep doing what you are doing, and God will keep forgiving it." That whisper is not the voice of Jesus but of Satan. Licentiousness is a way of "logically" explaining away sinful conduct in order to engage in many sins, including that of sexual immorality. It is a dangerous presumption on God's free gift of grace.

I also use *PIL* because to talk only about a very important topic like pornography can lead to a failure to connect the dots to so many other things. *PIL* is both specific to pornography while linking to broader issues. Each aspect of *PIL* helps us to see that the evil of pornography is not only limited to watching or reading explicit material. It situates it within *a sphere of activity that every sinner must face*, whether it be cultural or our own personal temptations. *PIL* also shows us that no one is immune, both to the factors that promote wide acceptance and usage of pornography but also to the danger of simply "going along to get along." Our apathy, though, is a threat to our families, communities, and congregations.

---

6. Rom 6:1.

Chapter Three

The Numbers Conversation
and What It Tells Us

THIS CHAPTER IS OBLIGATORY but uncomfortable. Sorry to do it, but I must mention some statistics regarding the viewing of and indulging in the *P* (*porneia*) in *PIL*.[1] We need to know the extent of the issue. The statistics cited refer to anyone who engages in visual and written pornography.

- 47 percent of families in the US report pornography as a problem.

- The average of age of first exposure is eleven years old; 94 percent of children will see pornography before the age of fourteen.

- 84.4 percent of teen males (14–18) view pornography regularly; 57 percent of teen females.

This is not simply a "them" versus "us" problem.

- 76 percent of young Christian adults (18–24) actively search for pornography.

1. Gilkerson, "Survey of Christian Counselors"; Cox et al., "How Prevalent Is Pornography?"; Webroot, "Internet Pornography"; Kingdom Works Studios, "15 Mind-Blowing Statistics." The statistics cited are an amalgamation taken from several agencies over the last three years. Things are much worse now.

- 68 percent of church-going men and 43 percent of *pastors*, watch pornography on a weekly basis.[2]

And it's not just a "singles" problem.

- 55 percent of married men and 25 percent of married women watch pornography at least once a month.
- 56 percent of divorces involve one party having an "obsessive interest" in pornography.

And it's frequent.

- 35 percent of all internet downloads are pornographic.
- 2.5 million Americans visit pornography sites every *sixty seconds*.
- One out of five mobile (smart phone) searches are for pornography.

I could go on; these numbers are but a drop in the bucket. Reflect on this though—how does a child of eleven see pornography? *Because it is everywhere and can be accessed at any time.* So, it's a technology problem, a parenting problem, an awareness problem. The pornography industry is powerful. It generates more revenue per year than the NBA, NFL, and MLB *combined*. It is a half a trillion dollar global industry, fueled by drug addiction and the sex trafficking trade of girls and children, *but also relying on the normalization of PIL.* Maybe now I've gotten your attention. Or perhaps you still tune me out, thinking, "It's not me, my child, my husband, my pastor." We tune out in part due to a lack of awareness. Or maybe we tune out in an effort to suppress our own guilt and shame. But many tune out because of just how saturated and normalized *PIL* has become. Ninety-four percent of men between eighteen and twenty-four *have a positive or neutral view of pornography*. Ninety-four. Women are increasingly watching more and more pornographic content. It is commonly and openly referenced in mass media. Pornography is prevalent in every aspect of the entertainment complex, whether it's streaming content, pop music, sporting events, or video games. Even social conservatives use the term "fear porn"[3] to refer to anything that is overly distorted. It's part of our normal language usage.

Wherever you find yourself, *it's always easier to sit in silence.* We've grown comfortable with silence. Not only have we have become numbed to

---

2. Maybe this explains why the church is silent on this issue!

3. Heard it from the mouth of a US senator just the other day!

PIL, Christians are more emboldened *by the silence of the church*. This has been my lived-out experience. I can think of one sermon in forty years of worship that even touched on pornography. The impression given is that it's not important enough to talk about or roundly condemn. Or it's only for those interested in the culture wars. But the numbers showing the effects of pornography tell a different story. The latest trend in education is to promote pornography as something that *should be* taught in classrooms in order that children might use it "wisely" and with "discernment." In one notable example, educator Justine Ang Fonte, a New York school teacher, was heralded for her sexual education curriculum that was "sex-positive" and called her lessons "pornography literacy."[4] What once passively seeped in is now being *promoted actively*. This goes hand-in-hand with all of the vile ideologies routinely shoved down kid's throats in the name of "education." It's called "porn literacy" and it's in even "red" states like Idaho.[5]

This is not a book that does a deep dive on the numbers or how our brains are being rewired by pornography and the internet. There are resources like that out there and I list several in the back of the book. This is not a book about the pornography business. Frankly, it's all too disgusting to mention the specifics. This is not a book about the outrageous things we come across every day.[6] This is a book about *root causes, root teachings, and then root solutions*. It seeks to answer the question, "How did we get here?" To call attention to the problem, how dire it is, but then to do something about it in the context of the church.

THE STORY PORNOGRAPHY TELLS US

Let's consider this in a different way. I've given you some numbers. I've sounded the warning. But think about our topic from the perspective of the *story* that pornography tells us.

God made us as creatures who delight in story. The Scriptures are two-thirds narrative, but besides the form, the Bible tells *the grand story of salvation of God's creation solely through the work of his Son, Jesus Christ*. We are caught up into this story, into this reality by faith, through our baptism. Our identity is imprinted on us through the story of God, the gospel. But

4. Safronova, "Private-School Sex Educator."

5. Sometimes these "programs" are cloaked in sex education classes. But explicit material and explicit language speaks for itself.

6. And that should be spoken against!

other things tell us stories too. Everywhere we look, we are given *an account of the world*. A complex set of events, realities, and circumstances that vie for our hearts. Whether it's through politics, movies, music, literature, social media, we are inundated with stories. I can sense you starting to scratch your head. "Stories?" Yeah, stories. How things are presented, how people frame the things that matter to them, what truth is conveyed (or not), what lies get told (and untold) . . . the particular view of the universe that is narrated through words and images. We are surrounded by stories. Many are harmful. Some are downright wicked.

So, what story does pornography tell? It tells us that intimacy is not intimate. It tells us that there is nothing more important than the indulgence of physical pleasure. It tells us that sex is a desire that is "taken care of" apart from a lifelong relationship between a man and woman in marriage. That the only thing that matters is the satiation of the self and inclination of the flesh. Nothing is too deviant or perverse. Anything goes. The ultimate purpose in life is the fulfillment of desires. People are disposable and expendable, as are their sexual experiences. This is the story told again and again to millions of people. Many of whom are Christians. And this story makes deep impressions on our psyches. Even to those who aren't directly engaging, this story pervades nearly every aspect of our lives. The story of the sexually immoral self has become the dominant narrative in our society. How did this story become so prevalent, even to ones who have had little or no direct exposure to pornography?

Chapter Four

The Cultural Conversation
Normalization and Saturation of *PIL*

Satan's intention is always to pervert what is good in the creation. He cannot create *ex nihilo* (from nothing); only God can do that. But what Satan can do is *twist what is a created good into something evil*. On the flip side, he also takes what is abominable and makes it seem palatable, what is abnormal and make it appear "the way it's supposed to be." And Satan uses our sinful nature to do his bidding, whether we recognize it or not. For those of you over a certain age, look back at your lifetime; think about what *used to be* forbidden and observe what *is now* commonly practiced. We know deep down this is not due to "progress" or "evolution," but due to *a normalization of what was once regarded as sin*. In fact, our entire culture has been so saturated by *PIL*,[1] including the people in the pews, that we have grown silent on many things.

LANGUAGE GAMES

One way this has happened is through the adoption of "better sounding" language. Take the example of two people living together outside of marriage. This used to be routinely condemned. We can see the progression

---

1. Remember that *PIL* is *porneia* (sexual perversion including pornography), general *im*morality (which allows for a whole range of behavior not God-pleasing), and *licen*tiousness (living in freedom from any constraint).

of our language in the progression of the practice. What used to be called "living in sin" has become known as "living together." We use the term "co-habitation," which is part of the problem. It sounds clinical and sterilized, scrubbed clean of any sinful connotations. Maybe we should just say it—you are living in sin! So, people "live together" and that now is counted as being married, when clearly it's not. That's just one example of how *language obfuscates sinful behavior*, making sin seem normal. Language can soft sell sin better than a teenager serving soft serve at a Dairy Queen.

How about language that does not necessarily signify sin, but is unclear? Take the example of "partner." Partner is now commonly used in place of married spouses. But partner *can* include other iterations of "marriage," including co-habitators. It linguistically works for a same-sex couple. Partner frequently appears in corporate training videos to pinch-hit for husbands/wives. But is being a "partner" really what being a husband and wife is all about? Some of you might say, "Of course! We are equal partners in our marriage. We share everything." That may be (I suspect marriage has been taught this way for decades), but *partner* allows for other configurations without overtly mentioning *a biological male husband and a biological female wife*. So, we should be precise in our language and not allow for ambiguity. Besides, is marriage just about partnership? Is it simply a "business arrangement" between two "interested parties"? I can speak for myself—I share my life, bed, and bank account with my wife, not my "partner."

Another way language obfuscates is by making everything a joke. As "living in sin" became more commonplace, so did the crass ways we talked about it. "Shacking up" became the humorous turn of phrase referring to two people openly flaunting God's desire. We laugh and shrug our shoulders. "What can we do? Guess we hate the sin but love the sinner!" . . . says every grandma who's ever had a grandchild doing something they know to be wrong. We turn things into jokes or matters of indifference so that we don't have to really confront what's going on. People who do deviant things, watch prurient things used to be called "perverts." That *meant something*. Now, perverts are quirky, part of the panoply of the many different ways to live one's life. Even the language of perversion has been changed into a language of inclusion. People are frequently told not to "kink shame" or that they should be "sex positive." It seems the last remaining "sin" in the eyes of the world is to actually call a thing a sin.

FIFTY SHADES OF GROSS!

Language, though, is but the symptom. The underlying cause of the normalization of *PIL* goes deeper. Before I went to the seminary to become a pastor, I worked for Barnes & Noble for seventeen years, ending with the position of store manager. In the summer of 2011, a phenomenon erupted within the book business. What was at first a self-published e-book became an international best-seller, bigger than *Harry Potter.* Seemingly everyone wanted this book, but no one could get it due to publication issues. It was featured on the *Today Show* as the "hot summer read." We got requests for it daily, going on weeks. Finally, inventory arrived. I was excited too; it represented a great sales opportunity to hit some goals for the store. The morning of its arrival, I opened up a case and took out a copy. I knew it was supposed to be some sort of "romance" novel. "Whatever will sell!" was my usual attitude. But as I stood in receiving, flipping through what would make my bottom line for the year, I was hit with a wave of dread. This book had no innuendo. No mystery. No romance. At all. My jaw dropped as I flipped through the pages. "This is pornography!" To be sure, objectionable content was and is easily found at any major bookstore. But this was different. It was beyond the pale. It was brash. Unapologetic. It was *explicit.* And I didn't want to sell it.

But I had a secondary concern. "My customers, many good Christian people, members of my congregation, are going to throw a fit!" I was dreading it—people who would call, write letters, boycott, and associate me with such *pornography.* I braced for the inevitable.[2] However, to my surprise not one single customer complained about this book. *Not one.* I even had members of the Bible study I taught on Sunday mornings coming in to buy it! It was the "hot summer read" after all! "Don't read that," I told one female class member, "it's pornography." "Oh, Chris! You're a prude! Lighten up." I was stunned. Then it hit me. *We have slid into Gomorrah and we don't even know it.* And I was personally profiting from the sale of this book. I felt convicted in my role in the whole affair. I left for the seminary not long after.

What does the story show? That *what used to be unthinkable* to publish, read, watch, and discuss *has become normal.* Ho-hum. Ordinary. There is no discernment (even by members of the church) regarding what is

---

2. To be fair, this anticipation wasn't without precedent. I had experienced pushback before.

pornographic, off-limits, and wicked. *Everything goes.* I remember vividly a grandmother-mother-daughter trio clasping their very own copies in the middle of the store, jumping up and down in their excitement! What were they going to do, have a family book club? So, we must be clear—*PIL* is a threat to our society and our congregational life together,[3] in part *because it is so saturated into our way of life.* And this is what it looks like—a grandma and her family delighting in what is so clearly pornographic. Really weird and gross. *PIL* is dangerous because it is pervasively *commonplace . . .* and no one wants to talk about it.

Concerning pornography, a quick word on the response I often get when I mention the topic. It comes in the form of a question: *What is pornography?* How do you define it? Sometimes people want clear lines and boundaries—what's in and out, black and white. But to wrestle over definitions muddies the water. While well-meaning people say they want clarity, I fear what they really want is a way to *categorize what is off-limits so they can feel secure in doing everything else.* "I don't watch porn; that's wrong . . . [same breath] Have you seen *Game of Thrones*?" To define pornography any more than the "production and consumption of sexual perversion" is certain to lead to a tacit acceptance of many other things. I put it bluntly—*pornography is way, way more than dirty movies.* Whatever definition one uses.

The "arts" have always pushed the boundaries with respect to sexualized content. During the twentieth century, there was a progression of *PIL* in music, movies, and literature. Elvis and his hips. Marilyn Monroe and her air grate. But you see the progression most in what was consumed on TV. Take the hit show *The Office.* Smartly written, well-performed, and very observant of culture, *The Office* is a show almost no one would deem problematic. However, many of its plotlines widely promote *PIL.* Any given episode features jokes about "hooking up," watching online porn, a distorted a view of marriage and dating, and much more. And America laughs. We laugh. Not a recent phenomenon though. A decade before, the megahit-show *Friends* actively promoted themes *directly at odds* with a right understanding of God's desire for human sexuality. It has enjoyed a resurgence in recent years, being introduced to a younger generation. Kids can buy *Friends* T-shirts at Walmart. A decade before that was *Cheers,* a show based primarily on the antics of a middle-aged over-sexed playboy who couldn't make a commitment to one woman, much less attempt to abide by any kind

---

3. I keep saying this over and over because it can't be said enough.

of sexual standard.[4] One can keep going further back and trace the wide acceptance of some form of *PIL* in one television era before the other. Even Barney Fife had a "girlfriend" on the side while dating Thelma Lou.[5]

THE DRIP

You roll your eyes. "You can't be serious! You're talking about normal television shows! They aren't pornography." Maybe you're not connecting the dots . . . or the drips.

I was recently listening to *The Suzanne Venker Show*. She had as her guest Joy Pullmann,[6] managing editor of *The Federalist*. Joy is a staunch advocate for children, education reform, and conserving tradition in our homes and world. She is pro-life, pro-family, and a Christian. But as Joy described, even though she came from a traditional, conservative Christian home (without television and with sparse contact with cultural ideas), she somehow absorbed the "feminist life script." This is the script accepted by millions of young women that tells them it's good to delay starting a family in order to first pursue a career so that a woman can "have it all." She had gotten married young, but didn't intend to have children right away, focusing instead on opportunities in her chosen field. She was going to follow the script she unwittingly absorbed. Then, oops! She got pregnant. Joy described being resentful at first, that this child would ruin her plans. She told the story with both regret and wonderment. How did these ideas seep in, ones so antithetical to how she was raised? In exploring this question, host Suzanne Venker termed it the "drip, drip, feed" of the culture . . . a drip that completely *supersedes* all that we presume is inculcated growing up in a Christian home.

This is what we've all had to face—*the cultural drip*. Like a steady IV line that feeds fluid into the arm, the world drips its stream of ideas into our subconscious, ideas that pervert God's good order and design, into nearly every single person. Whether it's through TV shows, the powerful influence of peers, or that "influencer" on Instagram who appears to have their life so together, we all absorb the ideas and practices that are out there.

---

4. Again, smartly written and acted, *Cheers* was a window into the cultural mainstream, while normalizing boorish behavior.

5. Juanita at the diner if you must know!

6. Venker, "Why the Feminist Life Script."

Because it's a drip, because it's slow and methodical, *we tend not to notice*.[7] But the drip happens to all, even those trying to insulate from what is obviously pernicious. And it's the drip of the seemingly "normal" that's most dangerous. The drip shapes our lives in ways we don't recognize. It comes in the form of so many things we consume on a daily basis.

A TALE OF THREE SONGS, OR "IS IT OKAY FOR A CHRISTIAN TO LISTEN TO PRINCE?"

To demonstrate the efficacy of the "drip," we turn to pop music. To be sure, there are *thousands* of examples of sexual perversity in modern music, but I choose instead three from well-known artists of my youth.[8] I am "one of the olds," but it turns out that music from my childhood (the eighties) is quite popular nowadays. Each artist selected is a *cultural icon*,[9] so much so that two are identified by a singular name. To underscore my point about the drip of *PIL*, indulge me as we analyze one song from each artist. Our first is a song that none of you would deem problematic: "Material Girl," by that paragon of virtue, Madonna.

You're quick to point out that the song is satire; its tone is ironic. It pokes fun at relationships between the sexes and is an obvious homage to Marilyn Monroe's "Diamonds Are a Girl's Best Friend."[10] Fair enough. Let us also set aside what we know of the Material Girl herself, her stated world view and reputed perverse sexuality. My basic point remains: What picture of men and women does this song convey? While not meriting some kind of deep dive worthy of a Dostoevsky novel, the lyrics call for analysis. The girl of the song (so, Madonna) is looking not for a man to marry, but any (many?) man (men) who meets one criteria—*they must have the cash*! She flirts and dabbles, but also sets the standard. *If you don't save your pennies, you will not make the Material Girl's rainy day.* "Romance" is bought and paid for. Double entendres abounding, the picture is painted of a tryst

---

7. It is the proverbial frog being slowly boiled in water by incrementally turning up the heat.

8. I was born in 1972.

9. This term is fascinating and deserves some explanation. Consider that an icon is an image or reflection of something transcendent. In many ways, "cultural icons" reflect the ideas in the culture back to the culture at large, but in a very alluring and powerful way.

10. From the film *Gentlemen Prefer Blondes*.

sought solely on the basis of *what wealth can be gained*. Presumably, once the money runs out, so does her warm embrace!

"A stupid, harmless song! The lyrics are vapid and trite. Why give it a second thought?" Exactly. *Why even give it a first one?* That's kinda the point. Music does this to us all—*it bores into our brains and hearts*. It drips into our veins. Music is pedagogically powerful in shaping worldviews, whether we recognize it or not. The *fact that I can sing most if not all of the lyrics from memory* (of a Madonna song no less!) attests to this. And I don't even like the stupid song! But "harmless" songs like this one promote a bleak view of relationships between the sexes, endorse the sin of lust and coveting, showing a standard of life thoroughly rooted in *PIL*.[11]

I can tell you're not convinced. Let's do song number two. You might concede that this one is a bit more troubling. "1999" was written by Prince Rogers Nelson or Prince, one of the most successful singers, songwriters, and musicians of the past forty years. A monster hit. I bet many of you have worked out or partied to it (some drunken revelry on the millennium eve no doubt). Try to set aside any sentimentality you might feel for the eighties (reflected in your Spotify playlist). Analyze what the lyrics *actually* say and the views they promote.

The scene is of Judgment Day. The singer (sung by rotating members of Prince's band The Revolution) seems to accept a day of reckoning is at hand.[12] Having a dream, the dream endorses a way of life; a way of coping with the imminent end. Instead of getting right with the returning Judge, however, *the singer is going to indulge the flesh*. The dream depicts "people running everywhere." There are signs of destruction, including a purple sky, but the singer *doesn't care*. The singer is a fatalist. If judgment's gonna happen, let it happen! There is a tacit acknowledgment that the singer is not in control; all of reality is cold and determined. There is only one thing the singer is interested in—*let us eat and drink, for tomorrow we die!* What the singer's going to do is "listen to the body." Let go of every instinct of fear and instead engage in carnal pleasure. Cause in the end, *nothing matters except having a party*. If I'm going down, I might as well have some fun.

Any Christian can see the problematic worldviews of both songs. Both Madonna and Prince were transcendent for their time. They were known by all. They exuded *PIL*, not just in their music, but in their public personas and private lifestyles. Both songs *center all of reality on the self and the self's*

---

11. Once again, *PIL* stands for *porneia*, general immorality, and *licentiousness*.

12. One begs to ask, "Reckoning for what? Who's the Judge?"

primary place in the world around—dead center. All that matters is that I have fun and have every felt need met. And people love these types of songs! They connect to some base, tribal, sinful urge to celebrate "the me." The other attending issue with so-called harmless pop music is that no one pays attention to what is being dripped into the collective consciousness of children. I speak from direct experience—parents then and now show little awareness of what ideas are being bored into their children's brains (or their own). Instead of practicing discernment over what their children listen to, the parents are singing right along.

I include one final song. It is, on one hand, a sort of post-mortem to the first two and on the other it captures the spirit of the present age. Billy Joel's "My Life." "I can't believe you are picking on Billy Joel!" You may wonder what this song has to do with our topic. To be sure, there is no explicit reference to *PIL*. Nothing sexually suggestive. The problem with this song is that it typifies in such a catchy way the pervasive spirit of *radical individual autonomy*.

The song opens with a call from an old friend.[13] The friend just can't do it anymore. Do what, you ask? "The American way." Whatever that is . . . I'm guessing a nine-to-five job and a conventional life? Jobs and houses lead to dangerous things like wives and children! Look out! You might have to take responsibility and provide for someone else! You might have to be a grown up! I digress. It seems the gentleman wants to be a standup comic instead. That's his passion. So, he moves to California and "he does him." Is there anything wrong with pursuing a talent or dream? Certainly not. But it's the refrain of the chorus that is most problematic.

We saw in the first two examples the center of the universe is *the self*. "So?" many of you respond. For this is how most everyone views the world—totally through the lens of "what's in it for me." The message that is dripped into our veins again and again is that *the self is the only thing that truly matters in life*. We live to serve the self at all costs. There is no outside arbiter, there is no external standard. "You can speak your mind but not on my time." Because it's my life. You do your life and I'll do "my thing." But where does God fit into this view of radical individual autonomy? What place does the Creator of the universe have in "my life"? Does God have any kind of say over how we live?

Within God's creation, the Christian is given an abundance of choices. In other words, God gives variety. The richness of the doctrine of vocation

13. Supposedly the comedian Richard Lewis.

shows us that we all have things we need to do (duty and responsibility), but also things that we *get to do*, even things that *we want to do*. My argument is not to eliminate the freedom of choice, *but to situate it within a dependance on the One Who gives us all things*. To align our "choices" with the One who is the arbiter of choices. Billy Jocl's refrain is *not* the final word regarding every single decision anyone makes. We don't get to choose what we do and who we do it with *irrespective of what God says*. Quite the opposite in fact. Our choices are governed by what God's word teaches and natural Law dictates. But our pushback (whether we realize it or not) is to say to God, "There is nothing you may say or indeed can say to me. I am the judge and jury. I do what I want to do. Whatever I choose to do within the privacy of my own home . . ." You've heard the tropes. But whether we articulate it or not, *practically everyone conceives of and lives their lives in this way.*

There's even a darker side to the fierce independence exemplified in songs like "My Life." It is the dark reality of not counting on anyone, not listening to anyone's counsel, not caring what anyone thinks about your life. *It is to live life alone.* Oh, you can be around people, but you can never have a real relationship. Radical autonomy demands at the end of the day that we "sell the house and close the shop." Who needs people to depend on and to depend on people? Who needs to express any vulnerability and actually pretend we "need others"? A life lived on one's own terms, at all costs, is a life lived apart from real human relationships. Pornography is another way that people become disconnected from other people and the reality of God-given procreative intimacy between husband and wife. Pornography is the sexual expression and imagination of the fiercely independent human, who does whatever, whenever. The self and its desires is that which are idolized. On-demand satisfaction. As long as my sexual needs are met . . . you don't need to worry for me "because I'm alright."

This promotion of the radical autonomous self presents a crisis for anyone who is a member of the body of Christ. For we are not free agents. We don't get to "bug out" whenever we want to or tell someone to "bug off" when they provide a comment on our stupid choices. And we certainly are not given warrant to live a life cut off from others while our every need is served on-demand. *We are beholden to the will of God.* We are also part of a community. We are parts of a body. We all have different gifts but are united by the same Head and animated by the same Spirit. We also live by the same rules. God's Law runs the show for the Christian. Again, God has given us stewardship over so many good gifts. We live in a country that permits a good amount of choice. But in response to Billy Joel's catchy lyrics—*it's not just your life and you don't get to do whatever you want*. It's actually God's life . . . given to you.

All of these songs in some way typify the American attitude toward the self and promote a perverted human anthropology. We view our bodies as things we can use for pleasure or utility or nothing at all, if that's what we choose, in part because we don't view the body as important. These songs (and many others) show us how we view our disembodied selves in the world. We see ourselves entitled to make any decision that we want. We are most offended when someone dares tell us "you can't sleep with somebody else" or "sleep in a strange place." But we are bound to standards and practices. We are, in fact, "slaves to righteousness leading to sanctification."[14] And no one in the body of Christ is free to engage in *porneia* or fornication or crass immorality. No matter what Billy Joel says.

14. Rom 6:19.

Excursus

Prudence

Perhaps you find these examples underwhelming (big yawn!), or you might even join the member of my Bible class in calling me "a prude." And I understand. I get it. When someone challenges views of the world that we have all embraced in some part, fed to us in our oatmeal, dripped into our coffee, a common reaction is to be dismissive. But let's take up the invective of "prude." Is being "hung up on sex" or overly concerned with morality a fair critique of my position? In other words, *are prudish Christians the real problem, as is so often claimed?* Do *we* even what know a "prude" is? Let's stop to talk about it—where the word *prude* comes from and how we might rethink the charge levied against me.

While clearly meaning something else today, the term *prude* is shortened from the one who "practices prudence." Whether from the French *prud'-homme* (good man) or the Latin *prudens* (to see forward), prudence has taken on a decidedly pejorative turn from its origin in recent decades. A person who showed prudence *was someone who was concerned with propriety and decorum and attempted to show wisdom with respect to conduct.* In the past, prudence served the public good. By contrast, a prude today has been distilled down to someone who is "uptight" or abnormally modest.[1] This is another example of how Satan effectively shifts the language, tempting people who are trying to uphold the good to feel as if *they are the ones in the wrong.* "Is it me? It's them, isn't it?" But perhaps in the body of Christ, there is a place to re-embrace one of the four cardinal virtues—prudence. Prudence is not only one of the four, it is the "mother" of them all. In other words, one can only be just, brave, and temperate *if they are first prudent.* Prudence isn't merely concerned with self-preservation, but with

1. We'll talk about modesty a bit later. Stay tuned.

the "perfected ability to make good choices."[2] Prudence is needed if "man is to carry through his impulses and instincts for right acting."[3] Prudence is man making noble choices, for the sake of what is good and true. Put another way: prudence is opposed to sin. All sin is "imprudent."

Maybe you're not yet persuaded. What does the Bible say about prudence? We focus on the book of Proverbs. The chief usage of "prudence"[4] is Prov 1:4–7. I give the fuller context:

> To know wisdom and instruction,
> to understand words of insight,
>   to receive instruction in wise dealing,
> in righteousness, justice, and equity;
>   *to give prudence to the simple,*
> knowledge and discretion to the youth—
>   Let the wise hear and increase in learning,
> and the one who understands obtain guidance,
>   to understand a proverb and a saying,
> the words of the wise and their riddles.
>   The fear of the Lord is the beginning of knowledge;
> fools despise wisdom and instruction.

Prudence is grouped within the things that the wise are to receive and give, *in order to fear the Lord.* Andrew Steinmann says that "in Proverbs [the words for prudence and prudent] signify the use of intelligence and wisdom to accomplish things that are aligned with God's will and that exhibit godly knowledge."[5] We see this later, where on the lips of Lady Wisdom, we find "prudence" her companion. "I, wisdom, *dwell with prudence,* and I find knowledge and discretion. The fear of the Lord is hatred of evil. Pride and arrogance and the way of evil and perverted speech I hate."[6] The goal is again the fear of the Lord, which is (in part) hatred of evil. In fact, the prudent man "sees danger and hides himself, but the simple go on and suffer for it."[7] To be prudent is to avoid harm and suffering, as well as to seek to do good.

2. Pieper, *Four Cardinal Virtues,* 6.

3. Pieper, *Four Cardinal Virtues,* 7.

4. The Hebrew word is *armah* and the related adjective for prudent is *armoom.*

5. Steinmann, *Proverbs,* 26.

6. Prov 8:12–13.

7. Prov 22:3.

So, if we were to be prudent, *we would be acting towards a thing that is good, and seeking to do that which is in accord with God's design.* Given the above, to be a "prude" then is *not* to be repressive, or restrictive for its own end, *but to promote something God-pleasing.* However, seen from the perspective of the evildoer, prudence is a threat! Hence the invective, "Prude! You're killing my buzz!" But from the standpoint of the sanctified saint bearing the Spirit's fruit, prudence is a guide and practice to do what is loving, joyful, patient, kind, good, faithful, gentle, and self-controlled. Is then being a prude a bad thing for society, for the family, for the church, for one's own life? Perhaps we need a bit more prudence.

Keeping the above in mind, I would ask you, dear reader, to examine your own viewing, reading, and listening habits. Is there something that pushes the boundaries of what you *know to be* immoral and contrary to God's will, yet you continue to partake? Have you made categories of things that are "mostly" acceptable as long as they don't cross some arbitrary line you have set for yourself? The fact is *we all negotiate the arts in this way.* Perhaps there is a discussion to be had about the lines we draw, but the basic point is that *our entire way of life and culture is steeped in PIL,* whether we recognize it or not. Maybe being prudent with respect to what we consume on a mass scale is not the problem!

Chapter Five

A Short, First Technology Conversation
Naming the Problem

A FREQUENT QUESTION I get as a pastor is "How did we get here? What has happened?" People are genuinely concerned about the outrageous things they see going on in the world. The answer to their question is complex, but it can be traced. In a book trying to get at root causes, I offer a short synopsis of how the development in technology has advanced cultural ideas, leading to broader acceptance of things once taboo.[1]

So, even though every manner of debauchery has been around since Adam and Eve were kicked out of the garden, the overall dissemination of *PIL* in our culture has exploded in recent years. What are the ideological and technological causes?[2] Multi-faceted. Since World War II, our country has lived in an age of tremendous technological advance. While creating wealth and comforts, some of these innovations have led to some disastrous side-effects. With the FDA's approval and subsequent legalization of the birth control pill in 1960, *the act of intimacy and sex was effectively severed from its procreative purpose on a national scale.* This "freed" people up (*licentiousness*) to engage in the act of sex without the "consequences" of a child. The so-called sexual revolution of the 1960s and beyond has groomed millions on the notion of "casual sex" with multiple partners. These practices have been ramped up in recent years with the use of the dating app

---

1. This could be a book in and of itself.
2. Technology is in part the delivery system for ideas.

and long-term exposure to the casual sex script. This is to say nothing of the effect of the "women's liberation movement" and the story that movement has imprinted on millions.[3] The bottom line—our culture has increasingly embraced *PIL* in many different forms and our technology has advanced it at every turn. The generation born after 1945 rejected the morality of their parents (the increase of *im*morality), with other generations following their lead, inheriting their practices and worldview. Cinema imitated the immoral life, and life was projected onto art. Inhibitions lessened over time and people became bolder in their perverted views of sexuality, without critically thinking about the outcomes. With the introduction of cable TV in the late 1970s and the home computer in the mid-eighties, people could now readily access *PIL* in the privacy of their homes. But it was the advent of the smart phone that gave anyone, anywhere, at any time access to *PIL*. Pornography on demand, 24/7. Quick, easy, and cheap.[4]

We used to hold meaningful conversations about the role of technology in our lives. When the personal home computer became commonplace, parents were instructed to keep them out of bedrooms and in a public area. They were told to limit children's access. Sound advice. But over the last two decades, these practices have been abandoned with the wireless router and the smart phone. Even worse, in the name of safety, education, entertainment, and "mom needs a break," seemingly every child is given some kind of wireless device to spend countless hours upon with little-to-no direct supervision. Now, every teen has access to whatever they want. I wonder what they'll look at?!

It's commonly asserted, "Technology is a neutral tool—neither good nor bad." Folks, technology, while inanimate, *is not neutral*. For instance, the "like" button used in social media platforms was invented in order to manipulate an intended response and more frequent usage. Not neutral! "Smart" technology is *designed to shape, mold, and track behavior*. While it may be a "tool," it certainly does do damage! So, phones in the hands of children and teens, in the hands of *everybody* gives all people access to *PIL*. Technology's ubiquitous presence has taken a toll on the way people relate to each other, especially with the opposite sex. Views of sexuality have been warped and twisted. Expectations are centered in the perverse "unreal" of what is viewed again and again. As a result, fewer people are getting

---

3. See the anecdote above in the section titled "The Drip" (ch. 6).

4. This includes any mobile screen technology or gaming system connected to the internet.

married (others delaying marriage), fewer people are raising families (or waiting to get pregnant). Gross, licentious behavior is skyrocketing. What started as curiosity has become something people cannot stop and actually drives expectations of sexuality. Titillation leads to habituation leads to addiction. Easy as ABC. Or *PIL*.[5] Driven by our technology.

This is but a brief overview and, for sure, scores of books have been written on many aspects of the aforementioned topics. We will return to the problem of technology later in part 3, where I offer some practical solutions.

5. Once again, *PIL* is *porneia*, immorality, licentiousness.

Chapter Six

The Modesty Conversation, or "That Young Lady Forgot to Put on Her Dress!"

WE TURN TO ANOTHER related (and uncomfortable) topic, but one that is necessary in our conversation—modesty. This is an overlooked discussion (especially in the church), so we have it here in some depth.

IMMODESTY ON FULL DISPLAY

We've talked about the degradation of standards and morality. *Nothing exemplifies this more than in the way people dress.* Pastors see this as much as anyone, viewing ladies in worship, coming to the Lord's Table, wearing low-cut tops and short, short(!) skirts. "Don't look down!" pastors say as they distribute the Supper. Even "respectable" people dress immodestly it seems. And we all put up with it readily enough.

While I don't intend to litigate the complete history of dress, to make my point I only need mention one article of clothing—*leggings*. Known by a number of names (yoga pants, running tights), leggings in some form have been around for centuries as inner or under wear. But in the early twenty-first century, leggings became accepted as *outerwear*. I remember the first time I saw a young lady wearing leggings in public *without* any kind of tunic top or dress (and not in an exercise setting).[1] I was working at Barnes & Noble one evening, when I spotted a college student wearing light-colored leggings with nothing to cover the "unmentionable" areas of her body. She was browsing books in the front of the store. My first reaction was, "That young lady forgot to put on her dress!" I was stunned. Should I say something? I didn't want to embarrass her. And then it dawned on me: *she intended to go out in public dressed this way.* My next reaction was (as I kept staring at her), "There is nothing left to the imagination." Next it was, "Turn away! Stop looking at that girl's body!" But truth be told, it was hard not to stare.

More and more women have become increasingly comfortable wearing clothing that is form-fitting, tight, and revealing. Society has also become more accepting. And the male cheers. Developments in the "modification of behavior" happen slowly (the drip), only to be punctuated by sudden, rapid advancements forward. Or in other words—drip, drip—bam! So, while the drip is ever-present, leggings-as-outerwear is a "bam" phenomenon. Things are going along, steadily getting worse, but then *hyperdrive.*

Once again, the "prude" slur springs from your lips. "Why can't you let people wear what they want without judging them? Besides, if you don't like it, that's your problem! Who made you the fashion police?" We get a little touchy when our behavior is critiqued, don't we? Rather than from a position of moral superiority, I am attempting to comment on how things have gotten so far away from what God desires that we have stopped paying attention.

WHAT IT IS, AND WHAT IT ISN'T

So, let's start with being clear about what modesty is—*an attribute of beauty* and a *God-pleasing virtue.* Modesty is an aspect of God's teaching in the Sixth Commandment.[2] To be modest in dress is to protect beauty by covering the human body God created (especially women's) from eyes of people (especially from men) God has not given them over to. *Modesty is a blessing that enables one to present themselves to the world in a way that does not cause offense, sin, or lust,* and in this, modesty actually *accentuates a woman's beauty.*[3] Modesty is a gift of God, especially to women. For most of

---

1. It was noted by a colleague that leggings-as-outerwear actually came about with Olivia Newton John and her 1982 song "Physical." He might have a point.

2. "Thou shalt not commit adultery." This is the Seventh in many Protestant traditions.

3. There is even a call to be modest in marriage.

antiquity, modesty conformed to a higher standard. There was the "vulgar" and the expectation to not be "crass" or "immodest." But that's long gone. With the erosion of all agreed-upon standards of behavior, modesty has left the building.

And let's be even clearer: *immodesty promotes sin that leads to more sin.* Put another way—*sinful males are going to stare.* Men will objectify a woman in immodest poses, situations, and dress. Even Christians! I am writing to those who are forgiven in Christ, and presumably believe that God sets the standard for all human behavior. I appeal not just to a Bible verse, *but to a way of life that followers of Christ are called to walk.* I am also writing to sinners. All of us. However, when a woman is immodest, it is not a singular sin affecting no one else. When a woman wears shorts with a slogan printed across the rear, more people than just that woman are involved. Men will "read the slogan."

It may seem that I'm picking on women. I turn to men's role in modesty in a moment. But women, as the more vulnerable sex,[4] put themselves in potentially dangerous situations through the practice of immodesty. As stated, men are all too happy to leer. The signal sent to the sin-saturated male brain by a woman in immodest attire is "stare at me." It is an invitation, whether intended or not. It then can and does lead to other things. Sometimes with tragic outcomes. But the argument from a view of *radical autonomy*[5] says, "It's my *right* to dress however I want! If *you* have a problem with it, then look the other way!" But to put the onus solely on the man is ignoring *the gift of modesty.* Men *should* look away. But women are to "cover up." And men are to help women in this task by not looking. *But.* Women who dress in tight fitting or revealing clothing *are saying the wrong things to the world at large.* Five minutes ago, this was commonly understood. No one would have disagreed.

Modesty (like prudence) has fallen out of favor, even within congregational churches. Just as Christians ape the culture in books, music, and movies, they do so with clothing. Folks, the culture is far gone. And it's never going to swing back to modesty. So, *we have to encourage it* and *model it* in the church.

---

4. I actually mean to write that! Vulnerability is *not* a diminishment of a woman's worth, dignity, or value. See 1 Pet 3:7.

5. This is a fancy way of saying, "my truth" or "you do you." See the previous chapter.

LEGGINGS AS FEMALE EMPOWERMENT?

We return for a moment to my initial example. I was curious exactly when leggings became outerwear, knowing this might reveal something about my topic. So, I looked on Wikipedia. I found a sub-heading listed as "Used as Outerwear." Bingo! But I was astonished. The listing made a startling set of assertions, arguing for the girl's *right to dress however she wants*:

> Restrictions on wearing leggings is sometimes linked to "****-shaming"[6] or "body shaming," with critics noting that, ". . .not being able to wear leggings because it's 'too distracting for boys,' is giving the impression we should be guilty for what guys do.'"[7]

The entry shows how truly upside down and twisted our modern notions have become. The argument made is that restricting revealing dress is a *threat* to people who want the freedom to act as wickedly as possible! But consider it from God's perspective—the way one dresses is a window into who they are and whose they are. Either we behave as God's sons and daughters, or as slaves to perverse cultural forces that dictate "fashion" and "popularity." So, many people condemn what is good and endorse what is wicked, while the rest go along without batting an eye. Sometimes, it seems like Satan is winning.

THE NATURAL INSTINCT OVERRIDDEN

However, modesty is actually *a natural inclination* implanted in every young lady by her Creator. Modesty is a good and proper instinct, especially as girls go through puberty and beyond. Modesty preserves decorum and helps people escape from shame.[8] As we know, little girls are fed messages of immodesty from the time they can walk. The messaging comes from a highly sexualized culture that is *trying to normalize something that goes against that natural inclination.* Over time, this good natural instinct gets overridden. Stores and online shops sell almost exclusively immodest clothing (to say the least) for kids. Mothers and grandmothers buy these

---

6. A four-letter term for a promiscuous woman.

7. Wikipedia, "Leggings." The quote is from a piece in *Time* magazine entitled "When Enforcing School Dress Codes Turn into **** Shaming."

8. We see this in the aftermath of the very first sin, as God "covered up" Adam and Eve in their nakedness.

clothes or dress their children in the "ways of the world." Think of the whole "child beauty pageant" scene! Gross!

This overriding of the good instinct goes beyond just clothing. Currents of thought in society (found in curricula in public education) demand that young teen women have to learn to be "comfortable with their body." What does *that* mean? Comfortable to reveal it to the public at any time and place? Comfortable with everyone staring at them? Comfortable in sending the exact *wrong message* to anyone within eye sight? Or comfortable to engage in what follows from immodest dress—gross and base behavior? Society "shames" women out of modesty by saying they have "hang ups" about how they dress and act. And now we have *generational* immodesty, handed down from mothers to daughters. As noted above, who is buying the tight-fitting clothes, after all? Who allows the girl dressed provocatively out of the house? In what ways is immodesty modeled in the home? How does the girl see the mother dress (and behave)?

THE ROLE OF THE FATHER IN MODESTY

This is where fathers have to share some of the blame and *most of the responsibility*. The father knows firsthand how men think. They know how *they* view a woman in immodest clothing. So, a father is to train his sons to be modest themselves by not staring at a woman. They must also teach them how to protect a woman's modesty. See below. But what if the father has a daughter? Also responsible. This responsibility often gets punted to mothers. But the father is perhaps *the only male in the entire world who will look at their daughter with eyes of love*. So, he is responsible for viewing what a daughter wears and then responsible for telling his wife if there is a problem. Frankly, the mother might not see it. *But dad does.* If he puts himself in the God-given role of protector, then he will see the potential pitfalls. This might even stray into the realm of the uncomfortable, but too much is at stake. Fathers need to be involved in the clothing conversation. Catholic author Leila Lawler, with respect to choosing appropriate swimwear for teenage daughters, puts it this way.

> Have your teenage daughter bend over wearing her current swimsuit in front of your husband, if you are having doubts—make him observe. [Edited to say that she does not have to aware of his observation—but I stand by my insistence that he must observe her. He is the only man on earth who has only her goodness at heart,

> unlike all the men at the beach who have already observed her. . .]
> I think then you will have all the support you need. I hope so. This
> really is a hill to die on.[9]

This might shock you, that a father would look at his baby in such a way. But what is happening when our daughters dress immodestly (perhaps innocently enough)? Do you think the other men out there are "averting their eyes"? Do you think when I saw that young woman with the pale-colored leggings I immediately looked away?

WHAT DOES THE BIBLE SAY?

In case you think I speak from some personal crusade of secular prudery, I assure you that modesty is a thoroughly biblical idea and concept.

> [I desire] likewise also that women should adorn themselves in respectable apparel, with modesty and self-control, not with braided hair and gold or pearls or costly attire, but with what is proper for women who profess godliness—with good works.[10]

Just so you don't think St. Paul is the only apostle concerned about modesty, St. Peter writes this:

> Do not let your adorning be external—the braiding of hair and the putting on of gold jewelry, or the clothing you wear—but let your adorning be the hidden person of the heart with the imperishable beauty of a gentle and quiet spirit, which in God's sight is very precious.[11]

More than "proof texts," the above show us that modesty is rooted in God's good order and design. It fits within his plan for men and women. *It restricts in order to promote.* But promote what?

It may seem that modesty is only about managing negative behavior. But it's more than that. There is also a positive aspect—*modesty upholds a woman's value and worth, and indeed her beauty, in the eyes of men and society.* Wearing leggings-as-outerwear doesn't liberate women, it makes them slaves to the desires of men. It doesn't empower women, but makes them *more vulnerable.* Modesty is God's gift to women to protect their worth and

---

9. Lawler, "Emergency Summer Reading."

10. 1 Tim 2:9–10.

11. 1 Pet 3:3–4.

dignity in a fallen world. And modesty has a *fierceness* to it. It says, "You may not look! You may not ogle. That is for another . . . someday. But not for you!" Modesty precludes a man from looking on parts of the body reserved only for a "one day" husband. Modesty puts the woman *in charge of who she will one day give herself to*, willingly, lovingly in the beautiful union of marriage. Modesty doesn't make a woman less, it elevates her beyond a mere object of desire on display. Modesty promotes a woman's dignity, promotes marriage, and promotes a woman's beauty.

THE DUTY OF THE MODEST MAN

What about the man? Isn't he to be modest? Of course. There is no double standard. He is never to go around in a state of undress.[12] But a man's role in modesty is more rooted in his call to honor and duty. He is to show *discretion and at all times protect a woman's reputation*. We talked of this above with respect to fathers. Remember the example about the father and the swimsuit? That's the picture, except it can extend out into society. A woman's modesty helps the man act honorably. But it's *reciprocal*. A man's sense of modesty is to uphold a woman in the eyes of the world. He is to defend a woman's honor. A man's modesty is less about "covering up" and *more about stepping up*. He not only looks away, training himself in this practice, but also discourages others from taking advantage of a woman, even if she is being immodest herself. Man's duty is to be responsible for his behavior and to maintain and protect a woman's dignity—in all things.

What does this look like? What are some practical ways a gentlemen can be a gentlemen? Very basic. *Look at woman's eyes when speaking to her.* Women know when you are not and looking elsewhere. Be conscious of this and develop the practice of "training the eyes." Also, don't presume to enter into a conversation with a woman you don't know if she hasn't given permission. It used to be a man would never greet a woman unless first given a signal of permission (a smile or nod) and even then it was a "hat tip" at the most. We are way beyond that now! But men can still be *deferential and take cues from a woman before approaching her*. And if a woman is in a state of immodest dress? Then do your best to avoid temptation. Be polite and kind, but disengage. This isn't rocket science. It just takes a bit of courage to do the right thing and go against the societal norms. It used to be called chivalry.

12. Besides, women don't want to see "that" anyway!

But perhaps, there may be situations where a man *might* say something. Not to embarrass, but to encourage and promote something good. It depends on your relationship with that particular person, but a quiet word to encourage someone to wear more appropriate clothing might be needed. And if other men are staring at a woman, a man might even need to interfere. Say something. Do something. Don't let men take advantage of women. Do we just keep our heads down and let wickedness happen? May it not be so!

I realize that to some of you this might seem incredibly . . . what's the word . . . *sexist*. "You are a patriarchal chauvinist pig." I assure you, I write out of a sense of pastoral obligation and kindness. But perhaps we should examine some of the modern tropes like "sexist" and "chauvinist" and "misogynist." Maybe the way we've been carrying on and labeling men isn't for the best. Those of you that find me "sexist," I ask, "What am I seeking to uphold and what are you seeking to defend?" And just what is "sexist" anyway? If it means that *I hold to the biological distinction between male and female*, that *both sexes are equal in dignity and value* but *have different roles and responsibilities*, and that *God's good order and design are to be upheld in the church* . . . then, yeah. Call me a "sexist."

TYING IT TO *PIL*

This can be confusing. How do I know what to do and when to do it? What is a good overall standard, even with respect to how we dress and behave? The standard is "whatever." As in whatever we want? No . . . we might put it this way for both sexes with respect to all behavior—"*whatever* is true, *whatever* is honorable, *whatever* is just, *whatever* is pure, *whatever* is lovely, *whatever* is commendable, if there is any excellence, if there is anything worthy of praise, think about these things. What you have learned and received and heard and seen in me—practice these things, and the God of peace will be with you."[13] *Whatever you do, do the thing that upholds goodness, truth, and beauty* and be at peace with our Creator.

So what does modesty and dress have to do with other issues, such as pornography? Remember the narrower topic of pornography is situated within the larger domain of *PIL—porneia, general immorality, and licentiousness.* The weakening of publicly agreed-upon standards of dress is both a symptom of a lack of morality and a cause of the hyper-sexualization

13. Phil 4:8–9.

we see, starting as young teens. Girls dress provocatively, because that's what most teenagers are marketed to do by the culture. It's what they see on social media. Teens will also tend to push boundaries. They will look to see how far they can go. And many parents let it happen, because they both abdicate responsibility and are knee-deep in their own hyper-sexualized lifestyles. But the unveiling of the "female form" is a dog whistle to any lustful male. Both are at fault and both (the immodest dresser and the leerer) are accountable. Obviously, pornography takes things several steps further. So, another way of looking at this whole thing—pornography *has no place for modesty*. And modesty has no place for sexual immorality of any kind. An obvious point. For if women and men strove to be modest, there would be a lot less porn.

Immodesty, especially in dress but also in behavior, is just one among many ways God's creation has abandoned his will regarding sexuality and interaction between men and women. But, as we shall see, this is not a new event and is a piece of a larger puzzle.

Excursus

Appropriateness

Talking of modesty in dress also raises the question: What about the allowance for standards in dress *to change* without it being considered immodest? In other words, at one time it was thought immodest for a woman to show her shoulder or wear shorts. So what about now? May a woman dress fashionably and still be modest? Yes . . . to a point. And here's why. The lost companion alongside modesty is *appropriateness*.

Who (culturally speaking) decides what is appropriate? Difficult to pin down, but appropriateness has as much to do *with the setting* as modesty has to do *with the behavior*. Appropriateness looks at *what is going on* at the same time as *where is it happening*. Appropriateness is what is deemed suitable, taking into account the surroundings and people involved. An example. A young girl goes for a run. She might wear a pair of running shorts. But that same girl *may not* wear those running shorts to church or to the prom or the dentist. "Flag on the play!" you cry. "She should be able to wear them wherever she wants!" No, *she shouldn't*. Because what is appropriate considers the setting. It seeks to find a fit with *what normally occurs* and *what is expected*. Another example. Let's say a woman wants to take an exercise class at the local YMCA. It is not a co-ed class. It is taught by a woman for women, and is essentially an exercise class to improve fitness, flexibility, and core strength. May she wear yoga pants? Sure . . . but with a caveat. Is she modest in her behavior? Is she at any time in view of males (who might be working out nearby)? Are the yoga pants absolutely too form-fitting? Who decides? Many considerations. But what is appropriate is an important part of this conversation.

A third example. Even more specific. Let's say you are a swimmer, one who does so for exercise. You swim every day at the local indoor pool.

Do you wear a swimming suit? Of course. A proper swim suit allows you to exercise efficiently. Might there be some more modest options? Always to be considered. So, you would wear *an appropriate swimming suit that would help you function properly while swimming laps.* You next get out of the pool. Do you go dry off, get in your car, and go home without changing? Of course not. Now most of you can see the point. You would have a towel nearby, cover up with a robe or swim cover, go to the locker room, and get changed. The modesty conversation must include appropriateness. And what is appropriate always takes into account what is modest.

Chapter Seven

Sodom and the Ark as Conversations in the Church

At this point, you may be starting to feel alarmed. Maybe you now see what Billy Joel and yoga pants have to do with pornography. But you also might feel I am not talking enough about Jesus and the gospel. Remember the stated goal is *to dive down into the root causes that have led to this matrix of permissive promiscuity which has led to an overt acceptance of pornography.* Perhaps you're on board with my deep dive into root causes, but you don't see a way out. Hopefully you're not demoralized! Rest assured, Jesus is coming. We will also turn to a fuller *positive* response of the faithful in our call to action. But before the turn, we must be very clear about the threats we face. We must be sober and vigilant but also confident of where to go. To do this, we digress to engage in two historical accounts from Scripture, both familiar stories[1] that can teach us something more about our current cultural situation. The first one sums up our societal sickness and the second offers a hopeful place of refuge in the body of Christ.

---

1. Please know by "story" I refer to the form of narrative and do not in any way imply it is not true.

THE ALLEGORY OF SODOM AND GOMORRAH

In Gen 18, three men visit Abraham and his wife Sarah. It is clear that one of the "men" is really the Lord. At the end of the visit, the two other men are sent toward the cities of Sodom and Gomorrah, because, "the outcry [against these cities] is great and their sin very grave."[2] The Lord is determined to destroy these cities due to their wickedness. Abraham negotiates with God to spare Sodom on behalf of his nephew Lot and his family who live there, but ultimately, not even ten righteous people are found that the Lord might stay his hand.

The two "angels" arrive at Sodom. Lot greets these visitors with deference and shows them hospitality. While they make as if to spend the night in the town square, Lot insists that they stay with him. He knows of the danger lying outside his door.

> But before they lay down, the men of the city, the men of Sodom, both young and old, all the people to the last man, surrounded the house. And they called to Lot, "Where are the men who came to you tonight? Bring them out to us, that we may know them." Lot went out to the men at the entrance, shut the door after him, and said, "I beg you, my brothers, do not act so wickedly. Behold, I have two daughters who have not known any man. Let me bring them out to you, and do to them as you please. Only do nothing to these men, for they have come under the shelter of my roof." But they said, "Stand back!" And they said, "This fellow came to sojourn, and he has become the judge! Now we will deal worse with you than with them." Then they pressed hard against the man Lot, and drew near to break the door down. But the men reached out their hands and brought Lot into the house with them and shut the door. And they struck with blindness the men who were at the entrance of the house, both small and great, so that they wore themselves out groping for the door.[3]

We might see this true, historical account as an allegory for our modern age.[4] Let's decode it. Lot's house is a representation of a congregational

2. Gen 18:20b.

3. Gen 19:4–11.

4. An allegory is a non-literal reading of a narrative meant to convey a secondary meaning not made explicit in the text. To read something as an allegory is to derive meaning from a text that the author did not necessarily intend. An allegory, however, can be a faithful reading of the story by applying the dynamics in the narrative to another situation.

church within the body of Christ. The two angels represent divine messengers carrying the word and authority of God. Lot himself can be seen as a (faithful?) member of the church. The men of Sodom (young and old) are the culture-at-large steeped in *PIL,* promoters of every manner of vile perversion.

We also decode the story itself. The two are welcomed into Lot's house. So far, so good. Lot does welcome these bearers of God's word. But when the men of the city learn that Lot has visitors (=authoritative teaching of the church), they surround the house and demand that Lot bring these men out to them. Please note—the men of Sodom are not content to "live and let live." They will not tolerate strangers (=anything that goes against the "orthodoxy" of their perversion) in their midst! *Their goal is to take these men by force.* The men of Sodom seek to impose their will on them, characterized in a vile way.

Lot attempts to intervene. He goes out *to them.* He calls the rabble "his brothers."[5] He tries to reason with them. In this, Lot shows that he is at ease among them, even though he knows of their outrage. It is of note also that Lot *leaves his house and shuts the door behind him.* Allegorically speaking, he abandons the safety of the church and leaves the word of God. To seek some sort of accommodation, presumably to protect his guests, Lot offers a solution that is actually *an abomination of a different kind*! What he proposes is also indescribably vile. But the men of Sodom clearly show that there can be no intervention or accommodation. They turn on Lot quickly. No tolerance! No middle ground. The greatest "outrage" to the rabble is that Lot is perceived as becoming their "judge"![6] Nothing short of complete compliance will do. Of course, we know that nothing can assail the church of Christ. The men of Sodom are struck blind; God's righteous judgment pours down upon the wicked city. God delivers the faithful few left in a crooked generation. Even if only for the sake of remembering his promises to Abraham.[7]

---

5. This is a shocking part of the narrative, and is part of Lot's somewhat troubled portrayal in Genesis.

6. It has been my experience that nominal Christians and non-Christians alike will use Matt 7:1 as a rejoinder against every attempt to speak about God's righteous standard against immorality. I take up this question in full in chapter 16, "Being a 'Holy Hypocrite.'"

7. Gen 19:29.

THE LESSON OF BEING THE CHURCH
WHILE SITUATED IN SODOM

The body of Christ dwells in a world surrounded by an endless sea of hostility. But congregations, even whole denominations, can be compromised by trying to reconcile with hostile world views antithetical to God's truth. In an effort to appear loving and inclusive, people instead "leave their homes" and go out in order to offer some kind of reasonable accommodation. This might be incorporating the world's ideas of "gender" into the Creeds or Lord's Prayer, or turning explicit sin into normal circumstances of life.[8] As with Lot, when this happens, *congregations stop being the church in that place, at that time.* They offer one abominable solution after another to negotiate a truce or even appear friendly to a hostile mob at the front door. Ironically, in their supposed "love" for humanity, they stop proclaiming God's truth and his free forgiveness of Jesus to all. They might even make these accommodations in the name of "evangelism." However, the end solution is *an abomination of convenience, an accommodation to what is evil, and an incorporation of what God condemns.*

Like Lot and his family, many congregational churches long for some kind of connection to the world outside the door doomed to destruction. This is not a slight against evangelism to all people. It is true that the church must always proclaim the gospel. *But that does not give us license to co-opt vile ideologies.* Despite repeated warnings that the Lord's patience was at an end and final judgment near, we are told that "Lot lingered." Why? Perhaps after everything, Lot still felt the pull towards his "brothers" or old life. Maybe he hoped there would be something salvageable after all. *We all feel the pull.* The sentimental urge of the rock band we used to like but that epitomizes the wrong things.[9] The movie we can quote ad infinitum but know is trashy and not God-pleasing. That sin-ladened hope that if we just tweak some things from the outside world and bring them inside the church, more outsiders will be saved. They will recognize the things they like "out there" and come to Jesus! Perhaps this was behind Lot's lethargy. Maybe he thought there was still something redeemable from the culture at large. But sadly, Sodom had passed the point of redemption. Not because

---

8. An example of this is the move in many Christian circles to minimize the sin of lust as acceptable as long as the person does not act upon it, or remains celibate.

9. Consider the band Led Zeppelin. Their lyrics and lifestyles were steeped in dark arts, pagan magic, and earth worship, not to mention sexual licentiousness.

God's mercy is limited, *but the hard hearted sinner resists God to the point of self-destruction.*

This is why the angelic messengers had to grab Lot and his family and drag them away. "So the men seized him and his wife and his two daughters by the hand, the LORD being merciful to him, and they brought him out and set him outside the city."[10] The time has come for us to be dragged away from all attempts to syncretize a life of worship and faith inside the body of Christ with what people "tend to like" and what is popular. It is a fool's errand to think we can ever satisfy the mob. Maybe we should stop trying and instead repent and turn to the Lord for his mercy in order to be a clear witness to the gospel and a place of refuge from the evils of the culture for all people who come to us in repentance and faith seeking the love of Christ.

THE LESSON OF LOT'S WIFE

This is the detail perhaps best-known but least understood. Why salt? What did it mean that she "looked back"? Was she unable, like the Nazis in *The Raiders of the Lost Ark*, to avert her eyes from that which would destroy her? The details are sparse. Lot's unnamed wife, trailing behind, dared to "look behind her." The clear command had been given—*do not look back or stop anywhere in the valley.* But Lot's wife did so to her destruction. Allegorically, we might say that she is like so many, despite the repeated warnings, *who finally cannot give up the old world until it destroys them.* Instead of ones who "press on toward the goal for the prize of the upward call,"[11] they keep looking back to *what lies behind*, craving the old life, the old feelings, the old Adam. They think, "Maybe there is something after all for me in the destruction . . . maybe God will save me *and* let me keep my old life." *Maybe.* The word of the double-minded. The fear of the Lord is the beginning of wisdom, but our sinful hearts yearn for what it most fixes upon in the world. Maybe God will bless my family and still let me have everything I sinfully desire. Maybe I can be a Christian and dabble with *PIL* on the side. Maybe there is still a way to "sanctify" gay marriage, fornication, and abortion, and still have a "church" wedding.

Maybe I can stream whatever is popular with no discernment.

10. Gen 19:16b.

11. Phil 3:14.

Maybe I can put my "pronouns" in my byline because it's a work requirement.

Maybe I can rationalize my acceptance of my friend's same-sex lifestyle because I'm supposed to be loving.

Maybe I can watch pornography in private because "it doesn't hurt anyone."

This is the basic point—*we are living in Sodom and Gomorrah and we don't even know it.* The problems we face are everywhere and deeply imbedded into the lives of the people of God. The threats are at the door and even *inside* the house. But we are to repent and look ahead. We are to turn to the Lord in all things, and abandon those things behind us that seek our destruction.

THE LESSON OF NOAH'S ARK

With the lesson of Lot in mind, perhaps another scriptural narrative might help us see how we are to be faithful in the face of wickedness and how God has given us a place of refuge in the midst of the storm. While historically and narratively previous to Lot, God's judgment of the flood and Noah's response to God's word is a place where we can also learn a valuable lesson. But first, a little refresher on the story itself.

In the days leading to the flood, we are told, "The LORD saw that the wickedness of man was great in the earth, and that *every intention of the thoughts of his heart was only evil continually.* And the LORD regretted that he had made man on the earth, and it grieved him to his heart."[12] Folks, sin is serious! The question isn't *what kinds* of sins were being committed, but *that man's condition is only evil continually.* The Lord will not abide wickedness; indeed as a just God he *cannot.* In a verse that should give all of us pause, we are told that the Lord *regretted that he had created mankind.* With his righteous indignation, though, also comes a heart of sorrow. Sin grieves the heart of God. In this people ask, "Couldn't the Lord simply overlook the sin of mankind? Couldn't he put up with it? Isn't he loving?" No. No. *Yes.* The very nature of the perfect justice of God is not to "overlook sin" but to *do something about it.*

---

12. Gen 6:5–6 (my emphasis).

> So the LORD said, "I will blot out man whom I have created from the face of the land, man and animals and creeping things and birds of the heavens, for I am sorry that I have made them." But Noah found favor in the eyes of the LORD.[13]

In a creation saturated with sin, God seeks to remove it from the face of the earth. God also looks for anyone whom he might spare, anyone who trusts in him and his word. And the Lord finds him—Noah. Noah found favor, or grace, in the sight of the Lord. The Lord viewed Noah differently. As the narrative unfolds, one sees why. The Lord gave Noah specific commands and instructions. Noah was repeatedly obedient to the word of the Lord. *He walked with God.* He did all that the Lord commanded him. But more than that, Noah trusted in God's Word of judgment and promise. In other words, *Noah had faith.* So, by grace through faith, he built the ark, he stored the food, he gathered the animals. But this took time. In fact, Noah was five hundred years old (5:32) when he began constructing the ark and six hundred years old when Noah was shut in. One hundred years pass! *All this time*, faithful Noah worked, obeying God's commands, trusting in his mercy to deliver him. But presumably, all this time Noah also proclaimed God's word. *The very act of building the ark is a living testimony to the world of his obedience to God.* We are not told if Noah proclaimed God's coming judgment verbally (though it stands to reason he did). But we are told repeatedly that Noah did *all the Lord told him to do.*[14] We are told that Noah was "a righteous man, blameless in his generation." Does this mean that he was without sin? Certainly not! It means that Noah was a *follower of the way of God and trusted in his word.* Noah showed the obedience of faith. And it was reckoned to him as righteousness.

The ark built by Noah was God's gift, a place of refuge from coming judgment. The ark preserved the creation, gave life to Noah and his family, and enfolded him in God's provision and embrace. Now for the allegory. The ark is allegorically the church, the body of Christ.[15] Noah is the faithful people of God who reside in his church. Just as in the time of Noah, we too live in a time of great wickedness. *PIL* is all around us; God's faithful people are seemingly fewer and fewer. Many are leaving the refuge and sanctuary of the church. They are foregoing the protection of the ark and instead live

13. Gen 6:7–8.

14. Gen 6:22; 7:5; 7:9; 7:16.

15. Obviously, I am not the first to note this! There is a long tradition in the church to see the allegory of the ark as the body of Christ.

in and with the world. Judgment is coming. The Day of the Lord is near. The ark of God, the body of Christ, found in local congregations, is the place of refuge for God's faithful, where they are to turn in a time of storm, in a time of *PIL.*

If we take both of these narratives together, we might also see a call *to live in the world but not of it.* This is a well-known aphorism, drawn from Scripture. Lot represents the fruitlessness of trying to accommodate the world and work within the culture to try to change it through compromise. Noah might be seen as one who is faithful to God's command and follows the Lord no matter what. While both men are "in the world," Lot's response is to go out to the mob and reason with it. Noah's is to unfailingly seek refuge for the coming storm. Noah, though, does this while raising a family and in full view of his neighbors and community. Noah engages in commerce and lives side by side those who will be swept up in the flood. While Lot has to be dragged away from a rain of sulfur and flame, Noah stays the course and receives the Lord's favor for it, rescued from the tribulation of a watery judgment. While we are "living in Sodom," there is a place of safety and rescue given to us, that we might flee from coming judgment and be preserved by the grace of God. The ark represents the body of Christ in these last days. With this in mind, we now turn to the fulfiller of these Old Testament types and shadows. We turn to Jesus.

PART TWO

A Conversation with St. Paul about *PIL*

Introduction

So, on the heels of the diagnosis of part 1, we need a scriptural rejoinder, first to the problem of sin, and then, *in Christ*, to our proper response to temptation and *PIL*. When pastors tell people to read the Bible and follow the teachings of God's word, we are turning to the source and norm of all faith and life. Pastors need to follow their own advice. But perhaps it's too vague to just appeal to "the Bible." So, in the interest of narrowing the sixty-six books down a bit, we focus on a profound section of the Holy Scriptures. When talking about the reality of being in Christ, standing justified before God on account of Christ alone, having God's gift of grace (not a result of works), and now being called to live in-the-world-but-not-of-it, *we can find no better place in Scripture to turn to than St. Paul.* It's a bit audacious to pick merely three places in Paul (so many!) and presume to tackle the great apostle (so many better qualified than I!), but let's give it a try. Each example looks at an aspect relevant to the discussion and gives solid grounding in both God's Law and Gospel to respond to *PIL* and consider the sin of pornography. To summarize the goal and aim in this section, consider Titus 2:11–14.

> For the grace of God has appeared, bringing salvation for all people, training us to renounce ungodliness and worldly passions, and to live self-controlled, upright, and godly lives in the present age, waiting for our blessed hope, the appearing of the glory of our great God and Savior Jesus Christ, who gave himself for us to

redeem us from all lawlessness and to purify for himself a people
for his own possession who are zealous for good works.

52

Chapter Eight

Colossians 2 and 3
The Indicative and the Imperative

PAUL ADDRESSES, TIME AND again, the Christian's current reality of *simul iustus et peccator*,[1] so relevant to this discussion. Many sections of Paul's letters are structured as if-then's—*if* you are found in Christ freely by his grace and work, *then* your response is to be that of Spirit-producing action. While many abound, I pick three pieces of Paul's corpus to highlight this dynamic and give us a proper footing. It is this identity, ones who are in Christ, that lays the groundwork for a God-pleasing Christian response to the threat of *PIL*.

Our first stop is the letter to the Colossians. Nothing demonstrates the if-then dynamic better than chapters 2 and 3. Paul, in the same near context, proclaims clearly that our salvation and redemption is *due to Jesus Christ alone*, and then seemingly in the very next breath, moves to concrete language that focuses on our lived-out response. So, first the gospel. Meditate on the words of Col 2:11–15 (the emphasis is mine):

> In him also you were circumcised with a circumcision made without hands, *by putting off the body of the flesh, by the circumcision of Christ, having been buried with him in baptism, in which you were also raised with him through faith in the powerful working of God, who raised him from the dead.* And you, who were dead in your trespasses and the uncircumcision of your flesh, *God made alive*

1. "Same time just and sinner," a classic Lutheran formulation of the tension in the Christian's life.

> *together with him, having forgiven us all our trespasses, by cancel-*
> *ing the record of debt that stood against us with its legal demands.*
> This he set aside, *nailing it to the cross.* He disarmed the rulers and
> authorities and put them to open shame, by triumphing over them
> in him.

This is pure gospel, written to Christians, ones who have already "received
Christ Jesus the Lord" and "walk in him." By way of reminder, Paul earlier
warns about being "taken captive" by the ways of the world and of the flesh.
He reminds them of their baptismal identity, the "circumcision made without hands" and how in this, they have put off "the body of the flesh" and
been "buried with Christ." From the tomb of Jesus, Paul says that they are
"raised with him through faith in the powerful working of God." More than
a one-time activity, *this is the new reality* for those who "are alive together
with him."[2] To put an even finer point on it, Paul says that those who were
dead in "the uncircumcision of your flesh," God has forgiven all trespasses
by "canceling the record of debt that stood against us." The image is one of
God taking our every sin, past, present, and future, and nailing *it all* to his
Son's cross.

But Paul doesn't stop there. After addressing their particular situation
of falling prey to an empty philosophy leading to false worship practices
(16–23), Paul says this a few verses later.

> *If then* you have been raised with Christ, seek the things that are
> above, where Christ is, seated at the right hand of God. *Set your*
> *minds on things that are above, not on things that are on earth.* For
> you have died, and your life is hidden with Christ in God. When
> Christ who is your life appears, then you also will appear with him
> in glory. *Put to death* therefore what is earthly in you: sexual im-
> morality, impurity, passion, evil desire, and covetousness, which is
> idolatry. On account of these the wrath of God is coming. In these
> you too once walked, when you were living in them. But now you
> must put them all away: anger, wrath, malice, slander, and obscene
> talk from your mouth. Do not lie to one another, seeing that you
> have *put off the old self with its practices and have put on the new*
> *self,* which is being renewed in knowledge after the image of its
> creator.[3]

---

2. Martin Luther's teaching on baptism is worth noting and is drawn from passages
such as this.

3. Col 3:1–10 (again, my emphasis).

Absolutely astounding! *If* you have been raised with Christ, *if* your every record of sin has been canceled, nailed to the cross, *if* you have been buried with him, *if* you are raised with him . . . *then you are to do some things.* If-then. Paul switches from the passive voice (expressing the indicative active agency of God in Christ to us and for us) to the active (demanding the imperative from God's redeemed people). Seek. Put off. Put on. Kill it dead. What is first on the list? *Porneia* . . . heading a list of "what is earthly in you."[4] Paul says to "put off" the old and "put on" the new self, which is being renewed in the image of its creator. He does not equivocate, but speaks to the active Christian life, one of repentance and faith, that flows from the regenerate heart.[5] As we experience temptation and every manner of sin, *we are implored to kill it dead.*

This creates a tension. Paul in Galatians calls us to "live by the Spirit" and bear the Spirit's fruit. *The good that we do is the work of the Spirit in us.* However, the reality of the Spirit's work in the Christian life often gets misinterpreted as the basis for *not* exhorting good behavior and a genuine morality. Why exhort a good tree to bear fruit?[6] But Paul does exhort, often. Paul speaks *both* to our lives *before God as ones receiving his gift of mercy* and *our active lives of obedience to his Law in the world.* He speaks to ones who are in Christ, but ones who know the common Christian struggle of sin. One speaks of our inability to do anything to save ourselves, but the other to the responsibility we bear for taking action as it relates to our love of neighbor. One is passive; the other active. Both are generated and authored by God.[7] But Paul can speak to *both* the deeper truth and reality of salvation in God's work alone *and* the way we experience the world, being attacked daily by *PIL*. In other words, on account of Jesus and his Spirit, we are exhorted to put sin to death in our lives. So, we let the tension stand— *we are saved by Christ alone, but are called to active obedience.* This duality has profound implications for one afflicted with the temptation of *PIL*.

4. Paul regularly uses lists of this type which encapsulate every aspect of *PIL*. See Gal 5:19–21; 1 Cor 5:9–13; Eph 5:3–4.

5. So, Titus 3:5.

6. For a terrific treatment of this question see Raabe and Voelz, "Why Exhort a Good Tree?," 154–63.

7. In some Lutheran circles, this is known as two kinds of righteousness. For more on this important dichotomy, see Biermann, *Case for Character*, 105–33, where Biermann suggests three kinds of righteousness.

Chapter Nine

1 Corinthians 5–6
PIL Problems and Paul's Response

As we see, the challenge of living as Christians in a God-less age is not new, but ancient. Many of the problems that plagued the first century congregations plague the twenty-first century ones. There is no better place to see this than in Paul's correspondence with the saints in Corinth.

Corinth was a large, cosmopolitan city of the Roman Empire. It was a commercial harbor town, strategically placed between water routes leading to Asia and to Italy. Corinth had been repopulated by Julius Caesar in 44 BC. Caesar put freedmen, veterans of his army, with urban tradesmen and laborers in Corinth. It had a liberal democratic government organized into citizen voters, a city council, and annual magistrates. The citizenry had the right to own property and initiate civil lawsuits. They inherited a variety of different cultures as Corinth was at an intersection of many people groups due to its trade and location. All of this added up to a city that was "prosperous and self-sufficient" and made up of people of "trade, business, and entrepreneurial pragmatism in the pursuit of success."[1] Its religious pluralism, rooted in the Roman tradition, would welcome a diversity of worship practices. The Christian church(es) of Corinth at the time of Paul's writing were likely a small blip in a sea of pagans, though they grew to be one of the most important centers of Christianity by the end of the century.

---

1. Thistleton, *First Epistle to the Corinthians*, 4. Much of the description of Corinth comes from the opening chapter of this book.

The Corinthian situation presented a significant challenge to the neophyte Christian. *How does one remain faithful to Christ when all around you is perversion, a self-liberating focus, and pagan idolatry?*[2] This challenge might sound familiar.

Paul's writings to the Corinthians were situational. That is, he was addressing specific topics in a kind of order, all unified and dealt with under the preaching of "Christ crucified." Several situations are denoted by the heading "Now concerning . . ."[3] But many other topics are woven into the first letter. All can be seen under the major umbrella issue of "divisions in the church." One by one, Paul takes on each challenge, starting with the divisions over who was baptized by whom, the philosophy of the world vs. the wisdom of God (the foolishness of the cross), questions over human leadership, gross sexual immorality in the congregations, lawsuits between believers, sexual immorality again(!), marriage and divorce, the unmarried and widowed, food offered to idols, idolatry, head coverings (men and women distinctions) in worship, the Lord's Supper and its malpractice, the reception and practice of the spiritual gifts, speaking in tongues and disorderly worship, and the denial of the resurrection of Christ and all the dead. Whew! First Corinthians is instructive to us because it is placed against a somewhat familiar cultural backdrop. We also can see how strongly Paul speaks against sin in the midst of congregational life. So, the question is: What does Paul have to say to us today regarding our problem of *PIL*? With this in mind, we look closely at chapters 5 and 6, starting with 5:1–2.

> It is actually reported that there is sexual immorality among you, and of a kind that is not tolerated even among pagans, for a man has his father's wife. And you are arrogant! Ought you not rather to mourn? Let him who has done this be removed from among you.

Right off the bat, we are confronted with an issue of *porneia*, a "kind that is not even tolerated even among the pagans." Paul is clear, but discreet—a man "has his father's wife." The presumption is that this is an incestuous relationship between stepmother and stepson. The first two clauses show us the severity of the situation. The construction gives an emphatic and outraged tone, that this unmentionable act is *truly, really heard abroad*. The issue, though, is not one "out there" but *inside the congregation*. So, how does Paul, as an apostle of Jesus Christ, handle this?

2. For a survey of the sexual perversity of the Corinthian and Roman context, see Rueger, *Sexual Morality in a Christless World*, 11–41.

3. See 7:1, 7:25, 8:1, 12:1. But there are many more topics *du jour*!

To use the phrase, sunlight is the best disinfectant. Paul sheds the light of day on their situation. Consider a moment how uncomfortable it would be to have this activity publicly addressed. To be sure, the Corinthians were well aware of the "situation," but Paul addresses it *openly*. Letters from Paul were not private correspondences; they were read in worship before the Supper and would serve as a sort of sermon. Can you imagine a pastor today preaching on something like this? Of course we can't; pastors are to "stick to religion" and stay out of people's business. The American view of the church. Instead Paul openly gets into people's affairs. Maybe the church today should be a little nosier and a little bolder in calling out sin.

Paul exhorts the congregation to remove the person "from among you" who has committed this act of *porneia*. This speaks to church discipline, something infrequently practiced in our day. Our American hackles are raised—who does Paul think he is anyway? But issues like this threaten the life of the congregation. They disrupt the community of faith and even one's standing before God. Verses 3–5.

> For though absent in body, I am present in spirit; and as if present, I have already pronounced judgment on the one who did such a thing. When you are assembled in the name of the Lord Jesus and my spirit is present, with the power of our Lord Jesus, you are to deliver this man to Satan for the destruction of the flesh, so that his spirit may be saved in the day of the Lord.

Church discipline is necessary so that the church might not be seen *tacitly endorsing the sin* and *the unrepentant sinner would be brought to repentance*. Such is the danger of silence on these issues by pastors and congregations—*sin goes unchecked and sinners remain secure*. In this case, in their arrogance, they seemed to be looking the other way. Paul says to remove such an offender from the fellowship. Not only this, they are to "deliver this man to Satan for the destruction of the flesh." What?! This can't be good . . . why would Paul say such a thing? Because sin is serious; *porneia* is dangerous. Left unattended, it can eat away at a congregation like a cancer. So, this man is to be put outside the sphere of the church and even God's protection, that *he might be exposed to the satanic, evil forces and his flesh would be attacked* (destruction of the flesh).[4] The hope is that this man is driven to repentance, would leave off with his wicked activity, plead for the mercy of God, correct or make whatever restitution is needed, so that he is restored

---

4. Consider again the admonition mentioned above to "put to death" what is earthly among us, the first of which is *porneia*.

first to the Lord in forgiveness, and then to the community in fellowship. For, as Paul says, this extreme measure is necessary that the man's "spirit may be saved in the day of the Lord." Falling prey to *PIL* can indeed have eternal consequences.

This may strike you as extremely harsh or judgmental. Remember the goal of church discipline—restoration. But this can only take place once the "old leaven" is removed.[5]

> Your boasting is not good. Do you not know that a little leaven leavens the whole lump? Cleanse out the old leaven that you may be a new lump, as you really are unleavened. For Christ, our Passover lamb, has been sacrificed. Let us therefore celebrate the festival, not with the old leaven, the leaven of malice and evil, but with the unleavened bread of sincerity and truth.[6]

Paul says their boasting (something like self-congratulations) is *not good*. A massive understatement! Paul uses Passover imagery to make his point. The "new lump" is a fresh batch of dough, activated with new yeast that causes the body of Christ in that place to grow in sincerity and truth. Paul profoundly grounds the entire discussion in the sacrifice of the Lamb of God, Jesus Christ. So, this "judgment" is necessary that the sinner be brought to repentance and restored, but also that the congregation might be re-established. The sin of one affects the many in the church. We struggle with this concept; *we view our sin as isolated and apart from anyone else.* This is one of the great rationalizations told in our contemporary age: *as long as it doesn't hurt anyone, it's okay to engage in sinful behavior.* We turn sin into non-sin with the self-assurance that no one is bothered by "what I do in the privacy of my home" or what is done between "two consenting adults." Standard tropes that amount to contemporary licentiousness. First Corinthians 5 clearly demonstrates that sin, especially of a sexual nature, is dangerous for a congregation. Looking the other way because we think it's none of our business is a great lie of Satan. Our boasting is not good.

Applying this to a modern context, consider how many times in congregational life two people get divorced. It's so commonplace we don't even bat an eye. But there it is for all to see—they stop sitting together, or one

5. Paul here is not circumventing or contradicting Matt 18! The presumption is that the climate of the congregation is accepting of this situation. Paul is calling all to account. In other words, if one brother would have gone to the other privately and addressed it the way Jesus instructs, Paul would not have had to address this in the way he does.

6. 1 Cor 5:6–8.

stops attending church.[7] If there is a day school, then even more people are publicly involved. Maybe one member transfers. Maybe they remarry other people of the same congregation. And we all look the other way. "Nothing to see here!" I've seen this first-hand. It is corrosive. It is hurtful.

Dropping down a few verses (skipping another situational topic), Paul addresses the issue of general sexual sin (*PIL*) and how God views sins of a sexual nature *differently* than others.

> The body is not meant for sexual immorality, but for the Lord, and the Lord for the body. And God raised the Lord and will also raise us up by his power. Do you not know that your bodies are members of Christ? Shall I then take the members of Christ and make them members of a prostitute? Never! Or do you not know that he who is joined to a prostitute becomes one body with her? For, as it is written, "The two will become one flesh." But he who is joined to the Lord becomes one spirit with him. *Flee from sexual immorality.* Every other sin a person commits is outside the body, *but the sexually immoral person sins against his own body.* Or do you not know that your body is a temple of the Holy Spirit within you, whom you have from God? You are not your own, for you were bought with a price. So glorify God in your body.[8]

Paul earlier summarized the above situations (the incidents involving the stepmother and son, believers suing other believers, and the general immorality of the present age) with quotations from the popular culture. "All things are lawful for me" and "Food is meant for the stomach and the stomach for food."[9] While not certain of the sources, most scholars agree they represent Corinthian *cultural maxims*. The first saying can be taken to mean simply, "I am free to do whatever I want."[10] A bit more cryptic, the second could mean something like, "All things are transitory and without any enduring significance." The modern man and present American context certainly embody the Corinthian spirit. However, our question should be: How does the Christian *of any age* view the body and what we are to do with them? There is no greater "sacred cow" in our culture than the assertion to bodily autonomy. Whether it's the proliferation of the tattoo, the rejoinder of "stay out of my bedroom," or the pro-abortion refrain of

---

7. Not to mention the "private matter" gets fully addressed on Facebook and Instagram!

8. 1 Cor 6:13b–18 (my emphasis).

9. Paul uses examples from the culture of his day to great rhetorical effect.

10. Leave me alone, this is my life; go ahead with your own life . . . leave me alone!

"my body, my choice," *the twenty-first-century human grows hostile to any talk of limiting behavior of any sort, especially if it involves how the body is used.* "All thing are lawful for me." Americans believe self-governance with no limitations to be sacrosanct, above any other dictum. But Paul tells his hearers, "The body is not meant for sexual immorality, but for the Lord, and the Lord for the body." This speaks to God's purpose and goal for the human body. It is the Lord who calls the shots! Our Creator has determined the proper function of the human body, and it certainly wasn't for *PIL*. But more than that, the body we believe to be "our own" is actually a body that has been purchased by another. Jesus Christ redeemed our very bodies (bought them back) and now owns them! This is astounding gospel, but it also signals *who* gets to have the say in how we use our redeemed bodies. Far from being transitory, our bodies are "owned" by another! As it turns out, we can't do whatever we want with our bodies, because they aren't even ours. We are stewards of something God holds the deed to.

Paul presses on to the cosmic reality of being joined to Christ. The logical conclusion of being a member of the body is that what we do with our bodies actually involves Jesus and the Spirit in that activity! This should give every single one of us pause. There are ramifications with *PIL* way beyond a simple issue of bodily autonomy. We are "joined to the Lord" and are "one spirit with him." Therefore, Paul says, *flee from sexual immorality*. Not navigate it as best you can, *but avoid it at all costs*. Run! As Paul reminds, the sin of *porneia* involves the Lord himself in the sordid activity. *The body is the dwelling place of the Holy Spirit for the baptized child of God.* Jesus Christ died on the cross to redeem your body back from the slavery of *PIL*. So, we are to glorify God in what we do with our total person.

One final note on this section: the issue of "judging others."

> I wrote to you in my letter not to associate with sexually immoral people—not at all meaning the sexually immoral of this world, or the greedy and swindlers, or idolaters, since then you would need to go out of the world. But now I am writing to you not to associate with anyone who bears the name of brother if he is guilty of sexual immorality or greed, or is an idolater, reviler, drunkard, or swindler—not even to eat with such a one. For what have I to do with judging outsiders? Is it not those inside the church whom you are to judge? God judges those outside. "Purge the evil person from among you."[11]

11. 1 Cor 5:9–13.

We are repeatedly told by the world that we must not judge another's behavior. We are reminded by non-Christians of Jesus's words to "judge not lest ye be judged." We are chastened by nominal Christians that we must not be hypocritical and we must love all people.[12] This a big, fat lie stuffed into the skin of the truth. And we have Paul on our side. Paul is dealing with a vile situation inside the Corinthian congregation. He reminds his hearers—do not associate with anyone who bears the name of brother (or sister) if he is guilty of . . . and he names several sins. That person is to be "purged" like "bad leaven" from their midst.

Where does this leave us in our own congregational situations? Are we to ignore open, manifest sinning by members of our churches? Are we to "look the other way" when we learn of two people living together outside of marriage? Are we to put up with *PIL* when it is present in our midst? While uncomfortable, I would suggest that we are to judge—*evaluate behavior based on God's standard and confront the unrepentant sin.* This might even escalate to the level of church discipline (see above). To be sure, we are to judge ourselves by the very same standards. How this might look is up to different church polities. But we are not to let immorality fester in the body of Christ. I realize this is complicated, and it's difficult, and you have all kinds of other questions about how this all works, but the bottom line is: *congregations (through the pastor and people) are to confront open sin that people might be brought to repentance.*

12. Again, I have more to say on this in chapter 16.

Chapter Ten

Romans 12 and Our "Next-Step Service"

Paul's letter to the Christians at Rome is his tour de force. For Lutherans, it is one of the foundational Scriptures of our Confessions. It provides the interpretive key for reading the Gospel books and proclaiming the gospel. Very often, the parts of Romans that are privileged (rightly so) are the first eleven chapters. But there is a noticeable and significant turn in the letter, and this turn is instructive for our topic.

In Rom 12:1–2, Paul says:

> I appeal to you therefore, brothers, by the mercies of God, to present your bodies as a living sacrifice, holy and acceptable to God, which is your spiritual worship. Do not be conformed to this world, but be transformed by the renewal of your mind, that by testing you may discern what is the will of God, what is good and acceptable and perfect.

First, what is the context? Paul has just preached the gospel in a rich variety of ways. He has assured his hearers that, although all have fallen short of God's glory and are sinners through and through, they are saved by God's gift of grace, which is received by faith in Christ. Christ has reconciled the enemies of God to his Father and is now the peace of the world. He says that his hearers are baptized into the death and resurrection of Christ and are now new creations. Christ came to save not just the Jew, but also the gentile, by the gospel, the power of God for salvation for all who believe. Chapter 12 comes directly after this doxology:

> Oh, the depth of the riches and wisdom and knowledge of God! How unsearchable are his judgments and how inscrutable his ways! "For who has known the mind of the Lord, or who has been his counselor?" "Or who has given a gift to him that he might be repaid?" For from him and through him and to him are all things. To him be glory forever. Amen.[1]

Given this triumphant conclusion to maybe the best eleven chapters in all of Scripture, one might think, "Sermon's over! Time to go." But wait. Paul keeps going. He begins a new section. *Paul makes a turn.* His tone changes. He speaks now more experientially and concretely. Verse 1 can be rendered thus:

> I exhort you, brothers, by the means of the mercies of God, to present your bodies as a living sacrifice, holy, pleasing to God, *your next-step service.*[2]

Your "next-step service." Paul, for the only time, uses the Greek word *logikos.* This has to do with what is reasonable, rational, with what follows consequentially. You might notice the English derivative *logic.* The common translation of "spiritual" is likely not what Paul has in mind. If Paul wants to say spiritual, he uses another word.[3] Paul's focus now is the Christian life of the believer, set free by the blood of Jesus, sanctified by the Holy Spirit . . . and then what that Christian is *consequentially to do.* What comes next.[4]

Two things to bear in mind. Paul wrote letters to congregations, who then heard them read aloud in worship. As stated earlier, they would function as a sermon. Paul's letters were also written to be read and heard in one sitting. In other words, what Paul preaches was *considered as a whole, in the context of worship, bearing the authority of the word of God.* What's the point? The hearers of this epistle, the Roman Christians, would still have the gospel ringing in their ears by the time Paul makes his turn to the practical. He begins to speak in a way that addresses the challenges of a Christian existence in and among pagans, but does so without abandoning

1. Rom 11:33–36.

2. Rom 12:1; my translation from the Greek.

3. *Pneumatikos.* Paul uses this adjective and related adverb twenty-three times (including three times in Romans).

4. This may seem like mere semantics, but Paul is a thoughtful writer. The phrase "spiritual worship" (ESV) muddies the water. So, whatever translation is rendered, Paul's point is to turn to a different way of speaking and focus in a new direction.

the gospel, what he just proclaimed for eleven whole chapters. This is very different from our experience. We get the Bible in bits. We might "hear" a letter of Paul over the course of several weeks of worship (if we go to church every Sunday!). Because Paul has spoken so clearly and exhaustively on the forgiveness of sins in Christ alone (not a result of works of the law), in chapter 12 and following, he now speaks concretely about the shape of the life of a congregation and how they are to live in the world. *He is exhorting works.*

This is eminently practical. Listen to what he next says: "Do not be conformed to this world, but be transformed by the renewal of your mind, that by testing you may discern what is the will of God, what is good and acceptable and perfect." Don't be conformed to this present age . . . instead, our thinking, our attitude, our thought is to be changed. The agent of this transformation is indeed the Holy Spirit, whose work was articulated beautifully in chapter 8; Paul now urges us to *take responsibility for our actions, our bodies, our lives, even our attitudes.*

> Let love be genuine. Abhor what is evil; hold fast to what is good. Love one another with brotherly affection. Outdo one another in showing honor. Do not be slothful in zeal, be fervent in spirit, serve the Lord. Rejoice in hope, be patient in tribulation, be constant in prayer. Contribute to the needs of the saints and seek to show hospitality.[5]

There are no qualifiers. No pulling of punches. Abhor what is evil. Hate it. Let it be a fetid, stinking smell in your nostrils. Note again the simple, concrete way in which Paul speaks. It's not overly sophisticated. It's so utterly simple that we tend to dismiss it. But he says, "That which is evil, which is contrary to good, contrary to God, contrary to his explicit will, hate it." In its place hold fast to good things. *Cling to it, be joined to it, stick to it like glue.* In rapid fire succession, he challenges the Spirit-possessed saint, the one who also still struggles with sin, to love the neighbor, be honorable in all things, be passionate and fervent in them. In all this, serve the Lord. Lest you think these are platitudes—overused trite sayings that have lost their meaningful effect—know that *we* have made them platitudinal in our dismissal of what is truly good and God pleasing. It's not the saying but the sinner who makes the platitude fall flat!

At the end of the chapter, Paul gives a sort of bookend to how he began—a simple directive aimed at the "what comes next service" of the renewed and regenerate Christian. *"Do not be overcome by evil, but overcome*

5. Rom 12:9–13.

evil with good." Sounds so simple! "Doesn't Paul know how hard this all is?" Well, certainly! Read chapter 7. Paul knows all too well the common Christian struggle.[6] I can't overstate it enough: Paul (through the inspiration of the Holy Ghost) knows exactly what he is doing and exactly what he has said! But he speaks in chapter 12 in a way that is not exploring the deeper theological truth of the gospel, but is urging Christians *to do battle against the forces of the enemy.* And the way evil is conquered (humanly speaking) is through the practice of the good. More on what that looks like for us in part 3 below.

In case you think I've forgotten about our topic, Paul has something to say about that in this section of Romans too. Just a little further down (13:11–14), he says this:

> Besides this you know the time, that the hour has come for you to wake from sleep. For salvation is nearer to us now than when we first believed. The night is far gone; the day is at hand. So then let us cast off the works of darkness and put on the armor of light. Let us walk properly as in the daytime, not in orgies and drunkenness, not in *sexual immorality*[7] and sensuality, not in quarreling and jealousy. But put on the Lord Jesus Christ, and make no provision for the flesh, to gratify its desires.

The language here is exhortative, intending to rouse to action. Paul reminds his hearers: *every day draws us closer to the Lord's Day of Judgment.* But now, through the power of God in Jesus, the power of darkness has been cast away! Therefore, let us walk, not in parties of perversity, not in dissolution, not in sexual immorality and sensuality . . . but *let us walk in decency, in what is becoming to a Christ follower.* All Christians can sometimes ignore these parts of Paul's letters, as if they are afterthoughts or "extra stuff." Paul has made a turn, not disconnected from the gospel and the power of the Holy Spirit, but directly flowing from it, pointing to a life lived that is consequential and what comes next in our lives of faith. The battle against *PIL* starts every single day in the life of a baptized, redeemed, sanctified child of God.

---

6. I treat this section specifically below.

7. This is a different word than *porneia* but is pointing to the same sordid activity.

Chapter Eleven

Three Lessons of Encouragement from St. Paul

We've looked at three case studies. I could have chosen a dozen others. But what have we learned? We have learned that Paul can both declare the gospel with boldness and clarity and still exhort good works as part of our Christian response. There is a consequential "then," an action required by the one who is in Christ. We have learned that Paul deals with specific situations in his ministry. He does not speak in generalities but directly into the lives of his hearers. Paul is also bold in dealing with the sin of *porneia* and in no uncertain terms condemns it. He appeals for congregations to "remove it" from their midst and not tolerate it among them. Paul sees that *porneia* is a threat![1] We also learned that Paul can speak in very concrete and direct ways that give people a phenomenological framework[2] to go about what comes next for them. Far from being a threat to the gospel proclamation, Paul grounds our lives together *in* the gospel, and sees what comes next as a necessary outflow. It is *God's will for our lives that the life of the Christian is to follow,* and our whole lives (bodies and minds) are in view in this Spirit-led endeavor.[3] Paul is able to speak about our topic not abstractly but

1. This of course is an echo from God's exhortation and warning to the people of Israel before they entered into the promised land, as we see in Deuteronomy.

2. A fancy way of saying "the way we experience the world and how we live in it."

3. In other words, the Law of God runs the show.

experientially, the way we live out our Christian existence with the constant threat and struggle with sin.

THE EXISTENTIAL CRISIS

Something else Paul teaches—he *personally* knows the "war that wages" inside of all of us. Paul relates to our struggle. He knows what it is to be "dead to sin" but still be governed by the "old flesh that lives within us." To know the truth of the Law, the abundant goodness of God's will, but still be seemingly powerless to fight against "the desires of the flesh."

> For I do not understand my own actions. For I do not do what I want, but I do the very thing I hate. Now if I do what I do not want, I agree with the law, that it is good. So now it is no longer I who do it, but sin that dwells within me. For I know that nothing good dwells in me, that is, in my flesh. For I have the desire to do what is right, but not the ability to carry it out. For I do not do the good I want, but the evil I do not want is what I keep on doing. Now if I do what I do not want, it is no longer I who do it, but sin that dwells within me. So I find it to be a law that when I want to do right, evil lies close at hand. For I delight in the law of God, in my inner being, but I see in my members another law waging war against the law of my mind and making me captive to the law of sin that dwells in my members.[4]

Scholars debate whether Paul is speaking about "Adam," or "Israel," or even the "rhetorical I."[5] But all of those explanations stretch plausibility. Paul speaks of his own experience, post-conversion, post-Damascus road . . . his own lived experience as a Christ follower. He knows what it is to struggle with sin existentially. He knows *our* struggle.

In this section, Paul speaks of the Law. But the Law *itself* is not the problem. God's foundational will and testimonies, found in Moses, indeed written in nature, are not the issue. *The problem is sin.* Paul relates to the common Christian struggle against "the flesh, sold under sin." The Law shows sin, gives it a name, and accuses every single sinner. So, we are confronted with death itself, as the Law shows us that the way of sin is to die. But Paul relates to the confounding war within us. It is "the sin that dwells"

---

4. Rom 7:15–23.

5. For a thorough analysis, see Middendorf, *Romans 1–8*, 584–97. I follow Middendorf's interpretation.

within Paul, within all of us, *that confounds us.* Paul relates to the feeling of wanting to stop, to not give in, to resist. But he knows how strong the urge is in all of us to allow sin to run rampant in our "mortal bodies." He uses the same "slave" language he employed earlier. In chapter 6 it was the *impossibility* of being a slave to sin for one who is baptized into Christ. But now *it is the experience of warfare within the person*, even the Christian person, of trying to *not* sin but still being enslaved to it. It is madness! We've all been there and so has Paul, wondering why we do the same things again and again . . . even after receiving the forgiveness of Christ.

To a Christian in the throes of a pornography addiction, this provides some comfort. Paul relates to the wanting to stop, to wanting to change. To do better. To break the cycle. If we really read along with Paul, he is confessing madness! How can this be? That the good I want to do, it's not what I do . . . but instead I do evil! We will take up this quandary in part 3, but for now, it is a comfort to know that we aren't unique or alone in our existential struggle with sin, especially something that can completely have us in its grip.

THE EXPERIENCE OF SUFFERING

Paul speaks not only existentially, but experientially. One relates to the problem of our existence itself, while the other speaks to our lived-out experiences we encounter. As a called apostle of Jesus, as his chief spokesperson, Paul *experienced suffering for following Christ.* Paul knew persecutions and every manner of affliction. This was not some theoretical endeavor with him.

> Are they servants of Christ? I am a better one—I am talking like a madman—with far greater labors, far more imprisonments, with countless beatings, and often near death. Five times I received at the hands of the Jews the forty lashes less one. Three times I was beaten with rods. Once I was stoned. Three times I was shipwrecked; a night and a day I was adrift at sea; on frequent journeys, in danger from rivers, danger from robbers, danger from my own people, danger from Gentiles, danger in the city, danger in the wilderness, danger at sea, danger from false brothers; in toil and hardship, through many a sleepless night, in hunger and thirst, often without food, in cold and exposure. And, apart from other things, there is the daily

pressure on me of my anxiety for all the churches. Who is weak, and
I am not weak? Who is made to fall, and I am not indignant?[6]

Not a #blessed moment. He is defending his work and reputation against those who boast in their own power and are trying to tear down Paul's apostleship. But Paul calls himself a "better servant of Christ" specifically because he too suffered many things—including real physical danger and hardship. Paul knew what is was like to be hungry, to be sleepless, to be threatened, and actually physically assaulted. While we may at times relate to this "human" portrayal, it's who Paul grounds it in—Christ. Paul says: "*If I must boast, I will boast of the things that show my weakness.*" For the weakness of attacks, of thorns in the flesh, is part of the Christian walk. We carry our cross daily, not to atone, but to follow our Savior.

We are never to chalk up our sexual sins to "I guess that's part of being a Christian." That's not the point. But we do suffer real hardship and temptation because we follow Christ. Suffering is to be expected. If it's not a porn addiction, then it will be something else. The Christian life is full of suffering, real suffering. While we can relate to Paul's existential battle, we might also relate to his real battle with suffering. We might also relate to Paul, indeed imitate him in his response and where he turns for help. For at the point of exhaustion and exasperation, whether it's the existential crisis of struggling with internal sin or real world physical dangers, Paul throws up his proverbial hands and cries out to God, "Who will deliver me? Who will deliver me from this body of death?"[7] He turns to the only place for a sinner to turn. *He turns to Jesus.* His Lord. Our Lord. Thanks be to God through Jesus Christ our Lord! Paul knows that both his thinking and the practice of his body are to be reformed and indeed changed. Paul also knows that for this to happen is to be totally dependent on Jesus Christ.

THE FULLEST OF ARMORS

There is one final stop in Paul that gives us needed encouragement. It is a passage that most of you will recognize: "putting on the full armor of God." For we must see the battle against *PIL* as not merely a culture war, or a fleshly struggle with sin. As Paul reminds us, *we struggle against unseen forces.*

6. 2 Cor 11:23–29.

7. Rom 7:24.

> Finally, be strong in the Lord and in the strength of his might. Put on the whole armor of God, that you may be able to stand against the schemes of the devil. For we do not wrestle against flesh and blood, but against the rulers, against the authorities, against the cosmic powers over this present darkness, *against the spiritual forces of evil in the heavenly places.*[8]

When we think of "spiritual warfare," what comes to mind? Let me rephrase: Do we *ever* think about spiritual warfare? I have talked about the role of Satan in *PIL*, and how actively our culture has embraced his perverse ideas. But consider that Satan and his minions are *attacking you.* Some of you might be put off by the "battle" language I have employed. It's too centered on "what we do." But I take my cue from St. Paul. For he says we are to "stand against" and "wrestle" the schemes of the devil and the spiritual forces at his disposal. To put on the "full armor" is to equip oneself for authentic, spiritual attacks. The war we face is real, but unseen. We might install a security system in our homes to protect from an intruder. What about the warfare that is a real threat, but *we can't see or touch*?

> Therefore take up the whole armor of God, that you may be able to withstand in the evil day, and having done all, to stand firm. Stand therefore, having fastened on the belt of truth, and having put on the breastplate of righteousness, and, as shoes for your feet, having put on the readiness given by the gospel of peace. In all circumstances take up the shield of faith, with which you can extinguish all the flaming darts of the evil one; and take the helmet of salvation, and the sword of the Spirit, which is the word of God, praying at all times in the Spirit, with all prayer and supplication.[9]

Paul is not summoning some sort of inner strength. He calls for the Christian to be armed with *the external gifts God gives* to undergo such attacks that will happen.[10] So, we "put on" armor or "let ourselves be clothed" in it.[11] The brilliance of Paul's assertion is that the Christian is being equipped not in their own might, *but in what we receive as ones "in the Lord."* It is the Lord who gives these external accoutrements, allowing us to stand and

---

8. Eph 6:10–12. My emphasis added.

9. Eph 6:13–17a.

10. See Winger, *Ephesians*, 700.

11. Winger, *Ephesians*, 700.

fight. Our trust is not in ourselves but in whom we cast our cares upon, "him who strengthens me."[12]

The full armor is the panoply, or the "complete equipment of a heavy armed soldier."[13] The Christian is armed to the teeth to withstand the devil's schemes. So, just what are Satan's methods? Several are named earlier in the letter. Paul warns of false teaching (deceitful scheming in 4:14) and the response to anger (4:26, lingering anger gives an opportunity to the devil) as two threats. But tying into our topic, I quote from the chapter earlier, where Paul says this (5:3–5, my emphasis):

> But *sexual immorality* [*porneia*] and all impurity or covetousness must not even be named among you, as is proper among saints. Let there be no filthiness nor foolish talk nor crude joking, which are out of place, but instead let there be thanksgiving. For you may be sure of this, that everyone who is sexually immoral [*pornos*][14] or impure, or who is covetous (that is, an idolater), *has no inheritance in the kingdom of Christ and God.*

Here we have Satan's goal in the attacks—*that the saints lose their inheritance in the kingdom of Christ and God.* Satan's schemes are to separate us from the body of Christ. This separation cannot come from a failure of God to keep his promises, or an insufficiency of Christ's sacrifice! But these threats are real and do happen. This can come only from our rejection of God's free gift of grace and a loss of faith. But Paul is clear: those who willfully engage in *PIL* unrepentantly are in grave danger. This is exactly what Satan wants. This is why he attacks. He uses *porneia* as one of his chief methods, that our faith might be undermined and our trust in God's sufficiency for our redemption is eroded. And this is spiritual warfare.

But our merciful God gives us his own armor in baptism to withstand Satan. Baptism is how we are incorporated into the body of Christ and how we are clothed. Consider then each of the six "virtues" given that we might stand firm:[15]

1. The Belt of Truth

2. The Breastplate of Righteousness

3. The Gospel of Peace as Shoes

12. Phil 4:13.
13. Winger, *Ephesians*, 702.
14. The related adjective to *porneia*.
15. See Winger, *Ephesians*, 728–54, for a full description of the armor.

4. The Shield of Faith

5. The Helmet of Salvation

6. The Sword of the Spirit=The Word of God

The whole body is covered. The corpus is protected by both breastplate and shield. The head is safeguarded by a helmet. The body is girded by the Truth, and for readiness, we wear the gospel as "walking shoes" or shoes for the road. But these are defensive weapons. The idea is not to attack Satan, *but to withstand him.* We are given only one single offensive weapon: the word of God, which is the sword of the Spirit.

As frightening as it is to consider the strength of the enemy, we are heartened to know that our Lord and Savior gives us more than we need to fight (withstand the schemes of) the devil. Our fight is to be covered in Christ and his righteousness and then to live in his protection. There are very practical ways this looks for the Christian life, whether that be at an individual level, or our life together in family and the community of faith.

PART THREE

The "Cure" for the Self, the Family, and the Congregation from Pornography and *PIL*

Chapter Twelve

A Conversation with the Solitary Sinner Trapped in *PIL*

THE FOUNDATIONAL FORGIVENESS OF JESUS . . . OR "THE CURE"

When one hears the word *cure*, one might think of visiting a doctor or taking a prescription of antibiotics. Undergoing treatments to fight cancer. A dietary cleanse of toxins or going to physical therapy for a bad back. All of those things, though, treat symptoms, but *a cure deals with the root causes.* So, a cure is to be healed, to fight a foreign invader, to take strong measures to be cleansed from an interior agent that is harming us. To cure a pornography "problem,"[1] the cure is grounded in repentance and faith, the "cure" for every single sin. *The cure for PIL and pornography is Christ.* This is best applied in private confession and absolution flowing from a life of worship. It is there that your pastor can hear your past struggle, your current burden, and pronounce the grace of God to you. It is there that you can find an ally in your battle against temptation for pornography and lust. It is there that your pastor can suggest some strategies going forward that can aid the repentant sinner to live a life of holiness and escape the cycle.

---

1. We might talk of a pornography "addiction" or a compulsion. This applies to someone who is seemingly powerless to stop viewing and engaging in pornography. But we are also talking of anyone who is tempted to engage, whether they are "addicted" or not.

Part Three: The "Cure" for the Self, the Family, and the Congregation

The cure is also the joyous living out of our baptismal life in Christ, a daily dying and rising. It is weekly or sometimes daily worship, a faithful reception of the Supper, the holy medicine of God for sick sinners. So, it is *in Christ alone . . .* and all that *that* entails, that we find the cure, the healing, the restoration for the individual sin of *PIL*. That is our framework for this entire discussion—*it is only through the redeeming blood of Jesus that we receive the cure of mercy.* It is through the sanctifying power of the Holy Ghost that we become regenerated and renewed to deal with the issues I have thus far raised. It is living lives of holiness, of piety, of charity, of chastity that we actively seek to "put to death" what is evil among us. In the forgiveness of Jesus, we talk now about how we actively wage war (living in accord with God's will and design) against pornography and *PIL*.

Doesn't *cure* denote something that goes away forever? Is it realistic to expect that one can be "cured" from ever watching pornography again? On one hand, the temptation is likely to always be present, even for one who reforms their life, in the forgiveness of Christ. We live in a fallen world, among fallen creatures, many who openly embrace *PIL* at every turn. *The temptation of lust doesn't simply go away.* This is the common Christian struggle we face on a daily basis. On the other hand, God can and does change hearts and habits. The Spirit bears active fruit. So, we live in a tension. The cure for pornography is rooted in the forgiveness of Christ alone, and it addresses the real temptations the sinner will (continue to) face. To put it another way: if someone is "cured" of cancer, that cancer can return. If someone is "cured" from a virus, the virus still persists to potentially return and take hold again. Until Christ returns and restores all things, we will still deal with the effects of the fall.

G. K. Chesterton famously quipped, "The problem with the world is me." If we are going to face *PIL* head-on, we start with individual sins and habits. And the logical place to begin our curing conversation is with the person trapped by weekly or daily engagement with pornography. Pornography addiction has been written about in some corners, but secretly treated (if at all) in the church. It is hard to pontificate on the pervasiveness of something that is to be kept (rightly so) within the confines of private confession. People are more apt to own up to an addiction to food, alcohol, or gambling than one of pornography. The sense is, even within the church, that pornography is not something dealt with routinely.

But there are many, many men (and women) who struggle. And *struggle* is the right word. For I write *not* to people who *don't* want to stop, or fail to acknowledge it as a problem. I am writing to Christians who partake of pornography, presumably who would acknowledge it is a sin, and who do feel a deep sense of guilt and shame because of their illicit habit. Many people are trapped in this sin. It has become a compulsion. In other words, their bodies, hearts, and minds are *trained* (habituated) to desire pornography, and they seemingly can't free themselves from the cycle. So, we want to consider (again, within the framework of confession and absolution) what the solitary sinner is to do to break the chains of addiction. What are some practical steps to take? What are some best practices to stop being addicted to pornography?

Many of these temptations come in moments alone, away from other eyes and people. The compulsion is strong. We've touched on the role of technology, and how the smart phone can give you access in a moment's notice. More on that below. But another challenge is that an engagement with pornography is also something that *most people are not likely to admit to*. So, when we condemn it (as I have done), we then invite people to seek help. We create a space within the body of Christ to confess it.[2] We emphasize that they partake of the free gift of God's grace in Jesus in holy absolution. We protect their anonymity, while letting them know they are not alone. We *then* give them concrete habits to replace the habit of pornography. We give people something to do in the moments of weakness. We focus on the power of the word and the power of "creational rehabituation."

You might have noticed I say "we." The sinner battling pornography cannot go this alone. So, there must be an ally or accountability partner. In the context of confession/absolution, this is the pastor. If it is a woman, the pastor might bring in another woman to assist him, such as a deaconess or woman working in the Christian community in human care. But there must be someone. People who try to kick it by themselves are likely to succumb to temptation. So, there has to be a "we."[3]

Some Christians bristle at this. "It focuses too much on our efforts." Let me be clear: *no Christ, no forgiveness*. No Christ, no transformation. No regeneration by the Spirit. But we must address *the very human element to changing habits and building new ones*. We are not merely disembodied spirits. We are creatures of God who live in a physical body. To say all that

---

2. What I say here is true of every sin, and not just pornography!

3. Matt Fradd's Strive: 21, a three-week detox from pornography, rightly emphasizes accountability. Any habit reformation or breaking of addiction program will always have accountability.

it takes is hearing the forgiveness of Christ has not broken the embodied cycle of addiction. There are other things at work. Imagine this scenario: A person comes to their pastor to confess their sin of pornography. They can't seem to stop watching it, even though they want to. The pastor pronounces the forgiveness of Christ. The person is grateful. He feels a burden lifted. The pastor's job done, he says, "See you next week!" The sinner trapped in old habits and thoughts is left a whole week to fend for himself. It's not as if the forgiveness isn't real or doesn't create a change. But there are real temptations, sometimes moment-to-moment, that the forgiven sinner faces. What I suggest below seeks to address the moment-to-moment challenges, all while proclaiming the mercy of Christ. This is in fact how Paul operates in his letters. Proclamation of the gospel, then employing concrete language to deal with the lived-out experience of the sinner.

PORNOGRAPHY IS A SPIRITUAL PROBLEM

Pornography involves the entire body. So, we need to retrain each part to "abhor evil and hold fast to what is good."[4] Consider the cure as a parts-in-light-of-the-whole approach. Each (body) part needs to be retrained and refocused, using the good gifts God gives us so that the person is reformed. With that said, pornography is a spiritual issue. So, what about the role of the Spirit in this conversation?

The Spirit works through the word and the means of grace. So, anything below that is suggested to cure the habit *is to be seen as the Spirit's work in bearing fruit in the sinner-now-redeemed-saint*. But to merely say, "The Spirit will take care of my pornography habit" is not a sufficient response. Not because it's not true, but because we are addressing an incarnational and creational problem (how we experience sin and the world) and that deserves, no *demands*, an appropriate incarnational and creational answer. So, the Spirit is living and active in the life of the Christian. He calls, gathers, enlightens, and sanctifies the whole person. At the same time, that person needs rehabituation of the body to turn to something good.

Lest you get the impression that curing pornography is merely doing a series of steps, or following some kind of checklist, let us be reminded that this battle is against the "schemes of the devil" in "this present darkness."[5]

4. Rom 12:9b.

5. See the above section "What We Learn from Paul: Putting on the Full Armor of God."

Therefore, we must view the battle against pornography as spiritual warfare. It is a battle fought against the "old flesh," but one that also takes place in the spiritual realm. Satan is undoubtably behind all that we see in the culture, and his designs are for your destruction. That is why it's crucial to see the Holy Spirit's role in creational rehabituation. Seeing it in this light also prepares us for the redoubling efforts of Satan to attack us. But be heartened! Christ is with you! His Spirit dwells within you.

CREATIONAL REHABITUATION

With this in mind, we turn to concrete actions, starting with the individual. In the power and name of Jesus, and by his mercy, I suggest: *something for the eyes, the lips, the hands, the heart, and the mind.*[6] My experience in counseling is that people *know it's wrong* and *want to stop* but feel a compulsion to engage (even after hearing the words of absolution). So, people need something to practice to replace the thoughts, inclinations, and habits of lust. I am not a clinical psychologist nor an addiction specialist. I am a pastor and a servant of the word.[7] My expertise is to "rightly handle the word of truth." So, I approach this cure both from the standpoint of God's word of forgiveness *and* the practical nature of how God changes habits through changing hearts and minds, in part by forming new habits. What I call *creational rehabituation.* This is using the body to recreate new practices by training it to do different things, predicated on the forgiveness of Christ alone.

Creational Rehabituation: Something for the Eyes

The eye is the lamp of the body. It both lets light in and reflects out. It is the gateway of what is consumed and a window into the heart, mind, and soul. Pornography starts with what is viewed. So, we need something for the eyes.

Determine the place where pornography is most often watched. Bedroom? Bathroom? Basement? Whatever the location, adorn that place with *an image of Jesus.* Put up a crucifix on the wall. Invest in and hang a painting

---

6. I greatly credit Pastor Scott Bruzek for his insight and formulation of this approach.

7. Full disclosure, I am also a recovered alcoholic and drug addict. I also draw much from my thirty-two years of sobriety.

that portrays Jesus, both in postures of his humiliation and his exultation. Artwork (beautiful art) has a powerful effect on the eye. In my office hangs a print of Titian's *Christ Carrying His Cross*. The painting is of Jesus bearing a cross beam on his left shoulder. Behind him trails an executioner urging him forward. On his head is the crown of thorns, pressed into the flesh, blood dripping down his brow. Christ's head is turned to face the viewer of the painting (wherever they sit!), revealing his right eye and side of his face. He is looking back at the sinner. His look says, "I am doing this for you. I bear my passion and cross for the sins of the world, *and also for your every sin and impulse*. Your every failing and failure. Your addictions, disease, and fornications. Your every thought, word, and deed." This painting is situated in such a way that Jesus looks right at me. Every day, all day. It is a powerful reminder to me of what I am to be doing in my ministry, for the people God has given me to serve.

So, what if you adorned your "den of iniquity" and turned it into a beautiful sanctuary, full of reminders of Christ's sacrifice and victory over sin? *Your eye would be confronted with this reality in the very place you go to the most to escape God's gaze and hide in your shame.* If there is more than one place, then adorn more than one. The eye needs to be engaged with something powerful and beautiful, a light of God's love that might penetrate into your consciousness, that the "eyes of your heart may become enlightened." In this new habit, the eye is trained to fix its gaze upon something meaningful in the very place it used to gaze on something else. Practically speaking, an image of Jesus is a deterrent against engaging in any sinful activity. The eye sees Jesus, and then is discouraged from looking at something that you know to be sinful and wicked. "Do not be overcome with evil but overcome evil with good."[8]

Creational Rehabituation: Something for the Lips (and Tongue)

This may seem a bit off. Why the lips? We don't watch pornography with our mouths do we? No, but our tongue is "a restless evil, full of deadly poison."[9] So, our tongues and talk can lead us down some dark roads. But our mouths can be re-tasked to help us fight *PIL* and the practice of watching pornography. With our mouth, we can pray (out loud) and recite God's word in moments of temptation.

8. Rom 12:21.

9. Jas 3:8.

Pray Constantly

In Luke 18, Jesus tells a parable to the effect that we might "always pray and not lose heart." The parable is about persistence in prayer, not to get things, but that in prayer we receive the reassurance that our Father hears us and he acts on our prayer. Prayer forces our pleas before God's throne that he might be moved to help us in our times of weakness. Prayer also trains us to deepen our dependence on our Heavenly Father. While you might have a regular time of prayer, I doubt thoughts of prayer are close at hand when engaged in *porneia*. So, we need to be retrained to call out to God in times of struggle. We practice "praying without ceasing." We start with phrases that get to the heart of the matter in the moment. Here are some very simple, yet powerful prayers:

> *Help me, Jesus!*
> *Be near me, Jesus!*
> *Give me strength Jesus!*
> *Have mercy on me, O Lord!*

These are short pleas that are to be uttered in the moment. You feel the urge. You feel the tug of temptation. You pray, "Be near me, Jesus." Maybe you repeat it. In this prayer, two things happen. God is in fact near you (for you are the temple of the Holy Spirit) and is stirred to give you reassurance of his presence. As well, the act of saying the prayer out loud trains *your body* (your ear is now involved) to resist the temptation until the moment has passed. Prayer can help you ride the wave. For many temptations are *merely moments*. If we can ride the wave out, we are able to move past it. Consider this. We've all been on a diet or tried to give up certain kinds of foods. The hardest times are those moments when you're not hungry, but when you're alone, and that cupcake is just sitting there. Tempting you to eat it. But if you can manage that moment, the craving can and does pass. Prayer both names out loud *what God does* and *gives you reassurance that he is in charge of your life.* Short, simple prayers can help to manage the moment when you are struck with the strong urge to engage in sin.[10]

10. I again am indebted to Scott Bruzek for this approach.

Memorization and Recitation of God's Word

But sometimes it's not just the moment but the overall lifestyle immersed in *PIL*. Alongside prayer (both regularly scheduled and moment-by-moment prayer), God gives us his word, specifically his written Holy Scriptures.[11] Memorizing meaningful Bible passages and reciting them out loud whenever your thought-world turns dark is a powerful tool against the enemies— *the sinful flesh and Satan*. Satan cannot abide hearing the word of God and God's name on our lips. So, put it there! Having a Bible passage at hand can be an offensive weapon against "this present darkness." The sword of the Spirit repeated again and again can counteract urges or times of fantasy. Even working on memorizing passages is a powerful rehabituation.

An example. I struggle with dark thoughts, usually about myself, my own self-worth. When things are going poorly, even in something as stupid as playing a bad round of golf, I have found that reciting Scripture in those moments *calms me and drives the troubling thoughts from my head*. The person who struggles with pornography can always shut their eyes, but they are left with the images in their mind. Scripture can change the interior conversation and evoke different images and focus the sinner on what God does in our lives. Imagine this scenario. You are thinking about the next time . . . where and when and so forth. You feel the rising guilt but also a level of rising excitement. *Your guilt is your cue.* Invoke God's name upon yourself. "I am a child of God." Pray. "Help me, Jesus!" Picture this—you're in your car driving. The thoughts are still there and reflexively you recite out loud:

> Have mercy on me, O God; according to Your steadfast love; according to your abundant mercy . . . blot out my transgressions . . . wash me thoroughly from my iniquity . . . and cleanse me from my sin.[12]

You say this (maybe the whole psalm) over and over again as a sort of mantra. It begins to take over your thoughts, but by way of your tongue. You train your instrument of "deadly poison" to instead be a means of calming the temptation and wicked thought-world you are fixated upon. God's word does things to us. It shapes and forms us. These aren't just general

11. The Word of God is Jesus, the preaching of Jesus, and the Scriptures that attest to and are centered on Jesus.

12. Ps 51:1–2.

truths but practical realities. Speaking the word and prayer can recalibrate the lustful inclination.

Creational Rehabituation: Something for the Hands

Clearly, there is more to this than what we look at and what we speak. We need something for the hands. For the hands are involved in this whole enterprise.

Lutherans don't use prayer beads. But in our tradition, we are encouraged in both the Small and Large Catechism to utilize a very powerful sign, something done with our hands that evokes and reminds.

> In the morning when you get up, *make the sign of the holy cross* and say: In the name of the Father and of the Son and of the Holy Spirit.[13]

> To defy the devil, I say, we should always keep the holy name upon our lips so that he may not be able to harm us as he would like to do. For this purpose it also helps to form the habit of commending ourselves each day to God—our soul and body, spouse, children, servants, and all that we have—for his protection against every conceivable need. This is why the Benedicite, the Gratias, and other evening and morning blessings were also introduced and have continued among us. From the same source comes the custom learned in childhood of *making the sign of the cross when something dreadful or frightening is seen or heard*, and saying, "Lord God, save me!" or, "Help, dear Lord Christ!" and the like.[14]

How simple! When we feel an urge strike us, we make the sign of the cross, as a reminder of our baptism, of who we are in Jesus, of what Jesus desires for us, as a reminder of his holy death and passion that freed us from our bondage and decay. We trace upon ourselves *with our hands* the shape and direction of our life in Christ. As well, we might start the habit of wearing a cross or crucifix. I like to wear mine under the shirt. Not to hide it, but to feel it press against the flesh of my sternum. *Pressing it down on my sinful flesh*, I make palpable appeal to the mercy of Christ. We make the sign of the cross, and then move to the center of our chest to imprint that instrument upon us, keeping our hands occupied for a few seconds in the moment of temptation.

13. "Daily Prayers," in *Luther's Small Catechism*, 30.

14. Kolb and Wengert, *Book of Concord*, 395–96 (my emphasis).

But what about work itself? Actually doing something with the hands? This is keeping busy and not being idle. Human creatures are called to work, produce, tend, keep, and organize. It is a simple admonition, but one that should not be ignored: idle hands make for the devil's workshop. There are many, many proverbs in, well, Proverbs that warn of sinful temptations arising from idleness. In considering the hands, we might see them as parts-for-the-whole and employ the entire body in work instead of boredom leading to temptation.

Creational Rehabituation: Something for the Heart

Very often the heart doesn't come up in this conversation. But what our heart fixes upon, our whole person will be oriented towards.[15] When I say heart, I speak of the *very seat of our being*. The heart is the epitome and center of all our desires. Someone in the throes of pornography has turned their heart away from God and fixed it onto self-pleasure. It could also be that the heart is longing for something, to soothe an interior distress or anxiety. Our heart looks for different idols that we might feel a rush of pleasure or escape from troubled emotions. To conquer the sin and habit of pornography, there is a need to redirect our heart away from these "gods" and train it to fix upon other objects. For where our heart is directed, there will our whole person be oriented. We head for what our heart is aimed at. In this endeavor, *worship is the chief thing to recalibrate our heart*. Worship plays a crucial role in creational rehabituation. Perhaps a bit more needs to be said about what worship is and what it does.

Put the modern notions aside. Worship is the place where God meets his people and dwells with them. Worship is the place where *God is present*. Worship is the location where God "delivers the goods." Many think of worship as an act we do for God. But worship is primarily where God gives us what he has for us. He gives, we receive.[16] We hear the pronouncement and forgiveness of sins repeatedly. After the invocation (God's name placed upon us), absolution is the first thing given in the "service of preparation" for the Divine Service. We corporately confess our sins and receive Christ's forgiveness. We respond to this gift with thanks and praise.

15. For a terrific discussion of this topic see Smith's *You Are What You Love*.

16. I describe here the Divine Service found in the Lutheran Service Book utilized by many in the LCMS.

But it doesn't stop there. We are bombarded again and again with moments of mercy. We hear the written word of God read aloud. We hear the proclamation of Jesus Christ and (again) his free forgiveness of sins in the sermon. We sing of God's acts of power and might and grace. We then receive *more* forgiveness in the Service of the Sacrament, God giving us his very body and blood (eating and drinking the mercy of God) for the forgiveness of all our sins. To quote the sainted Norman Nagel, in worship we receive "grace upon grace upon grace upon grace." *Worship is the delivery system of what God has to give his people, Sunday after Sunday.*

Worship is where the sinful human heart is recalibrated. It's where sinners go to receive God's free gift of favor, but also incarnationally, worship is where we experience God's grace. In this, through the power of the Spirit, our hearts can become changed. If the focus is solely on "my worship of God," we might see worship as something that we do, to (rightly) show our allegiance. But the sinner trapped in *PIL* and pornography might feel that he is not worthy to give allegiance or stand in God's presence. But if worship is primarily what God does and gives, then the heart is cleansed, changed, and transformed. Sick sinners need their medicine! Worship is medicine for the restless heart and soul, never at rest until it comes to rest in Jesus.

It's also quite possible that the person trapped in pornography doesn't worship or infrequently does so. If that's the case, then the prescription is: start today! Give your heart something to cling to and be shaped by. And it's not just the heart, but *all the senses* are involved. So, the entire person can be rehabituated through the act of worship. But at the end of the day, the most important thing any sinner receives from worship is the free forgiveness delivered to them. And in this the heart forms a habit.

Creational Rehabituation: Something for the Mind

The suggestions above are predicated in some form of the mind's renewal. This is the intentional acquiring of a different mind-set. It's the reason you're reading this book—*to possibly change your mind through engaging with different ideas.* Humanly speaking, we renew the mind by connecting with arguments that strengthen and edify. We learn and digest what helps us stay better informed. We pick up new insights and tactics. We come to different conclusions equipped with new facts. We change our mind through engagement with trusted resources. But we now focus more on the inner thought world. Not simply getting the facts, *but re-training how one thinks*. So, how does one do this?

To begin, we must be reflective enough to know what we think about most of the time and what triggers bring those thoughts on. We begin by paying attention. "What's on my mind the most?" This is being clued in to self-talk. In other words, what conversations do we have about ourselves? What do we tell ourselves? Is it negative? Is it self-loathing? Much of our self-destructive behavior is seeking to soothe something inside us, whether it be anxiety, depression, trauma, abuse. When dealing with addictive and compulsive behavior (such as watching pornography), one's inner dialogue can feed the behavior. So, we must flip the script, so to speak.

This is not done overnight, like turning off a light. But it does mean that we are aware (at the very least) of what conversations are in our head. The next step is to get out of our own head space and *get external*. We need to look outward for better thought patterns. We seek an outside conversation partner. The role of private confession and absolution is very powerful in this regard. You privately tell your pastor what is going on, with your body, with your heart, with your thoughts. He then can help with replacing old patterns with new ones, including how we talk to ourselves. What stories we tell ourselves. This takes time. This is painful. This is embarrassing. To say out loud what our inner thoughts are (the ones that help feed an insatiable lust, for example) is embarrassing. But let not that stop us! Instead, "Set your minds on things that are above, not on things that are on earth."[17] This, of course, is easily said, but harder done. But if the mind is not tended to, not just with respect to knowledge and new information, but our deepest thoughts, the body will follow suit. So, we have to get outside of our own heads, as with any sin, and look to the external things that God gives us.

17. Col 3:2.

Excursus

Accountability

What about accountability? I mentioned this earlier, but we need someone to help us on this rehabituation project. While God does forgive sins, and changes hearts and minds, while the Spirit forms and shapes our creational habits, we must embrace accountability. In fact, without it, people will fall back and fail. There needs to *be someone the person is accountable to, and things/processes in place that keep the person accountable.* In twelve-step programs, this person is called a sponsor. The sponsor is the one called in a moment of temptation. The sponsor is the one to call out the potential reoffender when he sees warning signs of a relapse. The sponsor is an accountability partner, who knows the struggles, who knows the particulars, who has a relationship with the alcoholic. Within the bounds of private confession, this person is the pastor. Because the pastor is the one who hears the confession, and whose ears are tombs (as it were), then the pastor can be the agent of accountability for someone struggling with pornography.

A pastor can be both an encourager and partner in accountability. We see this (again) with St. Paul. In Paul's letter to Philemon, a leader of the church in Colossae, he asks that Philemon forgive and be reconciled to Onesimus, a one-time slave. It seems that Onesimus had sinned against Philemon and run away. He then comes into contact with Paul, who became "his father during his imprisonment." Paul writes to Philemon on Onesimus's behalf, that he might have Onesimus back forever as a "beloved brother." He appeals to (rather than compels) Philemon on the basis of Christ and the love of Christ for one other. However, Paul also implicitly threatens Philemon with accountability. He says, "I write to you knowing that you will do even more than I say. At the same time prepare a guest room for me, for I am hoping that through your prayers I will be graciously given to you."[1] In other words, I expect you to comply with my request, *but I'm gonna check up on you to see how you followed through*! Paul knows both the power of encouragement and the power of accountability.

However, it isn't just the pastor. In the case of a husband, this person (one of them at least) should be his wife. How so? By being transparent with respect to all online dealings. This means sharing all bank accounts, having the same email addresses, and allowing the wife access to every single device he has. This means sharing passwords or using the same password manager. It means being upfront about what you watch and when you watch it. A wife can be a powerful prayer warrior for her husband, for she has the most to lose to pornographic indulgence.

For single men (and increasingly women), finding a network of friends who suffer from the same struggle is key. They might not be as hard to find as you think! There are many support groups all over the country and internet. There are also technological solutions that offer accountability. Covenant Eyes is one such online platform that offers an array of accountability measures—from screens to website filtering and more. Matt Fradd[2] and Strive: 21 is a terrific (and free!) three week detox program. Each day a new video of encouragement and empowerment is unlocked to aid on the journey. There is a robust community on the site to aid with questions and, yes, accountability. There are other online programs available to men's groups at churches and resources geared toward families. But alongside the technological accountability partners and measures, there is nothing as powerful as a friend who can hear your stories, pray with and for you, and hold you accountable in times of weakness.[3]

Accountability means that you are not alone. It means that someone else cares about you and wants you to do better. Accountability can also be painful and embarrassing. But it is necessary that we enlist the aid of someone to hold us to a higher standard. We can't do this by ourselves. God does not desire the sinner to struggle alone. Accountability is God's way of providing a check on turning inward and away from people.

---

1. Phlm 21–22.

2. Matt Fradd (mentioned earlier) is a Roman Catholic author and host of *Pints with Aquinas* who has written extensively on this topic. His book *The Porn Myth* displays the wickedness of pornography from a completely natural law argumentation. Accountability is a huge part of his approach.

3. I have more information regarding filters and accountability measures in the next section.

Chapter Thirteen

A Family Conversation
Blessing Our Children and Homes

THEREFORE, *IF THEN* WE are in Christ, we now turn our practical, experiential response to our topic toward the direction of the family. I am presuming (again) that those reading this are Christians, that some of you want to repent and amend your life, your habits, your minds . . . and that you want to do better as a husband or wife, a parent or grandparent, a brother or sister, an aunt or uncle, a son or daughter or neighbor. Maybe we ourselves don't have the particular affliction aforementioned, but you (are beginning to) recognize that we are responsible for the effects of *PIL*, and you ask, "Where do you go from here?"

We start with Jesus. To say it again, by way of emphasis, we must turn to Christ. Perhaps you need help and cannot stop indulging (see above). Perhaps you crave forgiveness for past sins and behaviors (that aren't specific to pornography) that you've never confessed. Perhaps you've made a mess and you don't know where to turn. Come see your pastor. Confess yours sins in private and receive absolution. Seek comfort in the forgiveness offered in the Divine Service. Worship the Lord and receive what he has to give, Sunday after Sunday. Eat and drink his holy medicine from his table. Seek professional help with a Christian counselor. And in confession and absolution, flowing from the grace God gives, in the power of the Holy Spirit, God changes hearts and habits. In the mercy of Christ and by his Spirit, our afflictions, our guilt and shame are overcome and we can get to work protecting our families.

Part Three: The "Cure" for the Self, the Family, and the Congregation

This section of part 3 looks at four basic components—*teaching, technology, dating, and parenting.* As you will see, these are not hermetically sealed categories. There is tremendous overlap and interplay. There also is not a lot of overt discussion of *PIL.* This section looks at foundational ways *that we keep it out of our families.* Think of it as tried and true approaches to not just combat *PIL* but establish the home and family as a location of the love of Jesus and a place centered on God's truth, goodness, and beauty.

I realize that the nuclear family I describe may not match your experience or current situation. We live in a time where the traditional family structure has been undermined at every turn. It has been imploded from within and attacked from without. But by "family" I mean generically *those people whom God has given you to be responsible for and to.* This might mean you are a grandmother raising two children because mom or dad are out of the picture. It might mean that you are a divorced father who has limited time with his children. It might mean that you are a young married couple who have no children. It might mean you are a single mom having to do both jobs as mother and father as well as having to work. Whatever the case, the below applies to every situation in life where one is directly or indirectly involved in the raising and training of children, whatever the logistics or configurations. But we all bear some responsibility with how the faith is taught and how *PIL* is fought against. With that said, God's "best"[1] is a biological husband and biological wife. A mom and a dad. So, whatever the family make-up, everything I say below in this section is geared toward that ideal. *Please remember I said this.* I haven't forgotten about broken or imperfect situations. I haven't forgotten about divorce. I haven't forgotten about the challenges of the fallen family structures we see around us every day. *I simply want us to aspire to what is God's best.*

With that said, we begin with teaching the faith, otherwise known as catechesis. For the best way to proactively fight *PIL* is by inculcating the word of God and forgiveness of Jesus into the habits and practices of *every single household.*

---

1. His truth, order, and design.

CATECHESIS THAT LASTS A LIFETIME—
AN INDOCTRINATION OF THE GOOD

Many are the plans in the mind of a man, but it is the purpose of the LORD that will stand.

—PROV 19:21

IT IS THE ONGOING concern in every congregation, denomination, and church body: *Where are the young people?* What has happened to them? Nearly everyone sees the problem—declining attendance, lack of participation in congregational life, the youth falling away after confirmation and not coming back. Maybe you have children, grandchildren, great grandchildren that are no longer attending worship. Maybe you even know of a family member who has never attended church (and has little interest in doing so). On top of this, in consideration of our topic, what are they being taught by the world? What practices and forces are forming and shaping them? What is the long-term effect of *PIL* on our children and families?

The question of "where are the youth" is not merely being asked at the congregational level, but at the district, synodical, and worldwide one too. And there are many approaches suggested and taken. One part of the equation is the need for evangelism. *People need to hear about Jesus.* But what about the people who have heard about Jesus but now want nothing to do with him? So, the part I seek to address is once they are here, *how might we keep them in the faith*? In other words, how might we catechize them in a lasting way so that they might remain in the faith? How might we make disciples?[2]

---

2. The answer is of course "baptizing and teaching" (Matt 28:19–20). But what does that look like?

Catechesis is a word one hears bandied about. It sounds technical and churchy and highfalutin. It simply means "the process of teaching the faith." It is derived from the verb "to sound back and forth." *To echo the faith.*[3] But it's more than teaching facts—*it's imprinting the faith in such a way that it leaves an impression.* Catechesis is not just acquiring knowledge, it is being formed and shaped by Christ and the Spirit in the life of the church. So, this subsection explores basic approaches to catechize people brought into the faith through baptism and evangelism, with a particular eye to the family structure (home life). The goal is to provide a clear set of practices that teach the faith in an enduring way. While what follows addresses children specifically, these practices apply to any age.

Again, why catechesis in the context of our topic? Because by failing to teach and indoctrinate our children, *we have handed over catechesis to the world.* Instead of being handed down the faith, they have been handed over to the culture at large. This is a general criticism, but one we all have played some role in. Until we take seriously our duties as parents, grandparents, pastors to intentionally teach the faith (and specifically what the Bible says about *PIL* and sexual purity), we will watch as we collectively slide further into hedonism.

Give Children (and All People!) Something to Grow into (and Not Out Of)

As children mature and grow, they move from certain things of interest to others. One year they're into a particular cartoon, book series, or superhero, and the next they're onto something else. In other words, children grow out of things. They grow out of shoes, clothes, tastes, what interests them. And when they grow out of things, *they rarely return back.*

In an effort to engage the child, many congregational practices of the past have attempted to be "kid friendly." While seemingly arbitrary, these practices share certain characteristics. Kid friendly ends up being cartoonish. Cheap. Plastic. Cutesy. An example: During a recent Lenten season, preparing for Good Friday worship, I noticed the children's worship supplement had a grotesque cartoon picture of Jesus bearing the cross for the child to color! We might not think too much about this most of the year, but this didn't sit well with me. Are we to reduce Jesus' death on a cross to a cartoon picture, so that it's "kid friendly" and they'll be "engaged"?

3. Luke 1:4.

Aside from the aesthetic, kids who use resources like this grow out of them. They stop being interested in coloring pictures or doing word searches. But the lasting impression made on the child (and the congregation) is that *the faith is something simplistic, cheap, and disposable*. A common assertion is, "Children need something that holds their attention." Fair enough. It is important to be age-appropriate. But does that mean there is nothing in the Divine Service, the sanctuary, or the season of the church to "hold their attention"? This is not only done for little children. It's done for the youth as well. Then the next level, and so forth. But where does it end? When does the child, youth, or young adult become enfolded into the life of the church with everyone else? Age forty-two after graduating out of the thirty-somethings small group?

The overall impression created in the child's mind is that "church is for kids." And when they're no longer kids, they look for something else. *What if we gave them something to grow into and not out of?* Consider this. Children learn to talk, not from cartoons, videos, or crafts. They learn from watching and imitating what they see and hear around them every single day. This is the way we are all "catechized" into our native tongue. So, going to worship, saying daily prayers, doing daily devotions, participating in the liturgy, attending substantial Bible classes . . . *being immersed in the life of the church grows us into and not out of the church.*

Related to daily catechesis and weekly worship (quantity) is what we feed our children (quality). Again, an example from daily life. Most any parent pays careful attention to what their children eat. We make sure that meals are balanced and nutritious. While we might give some variety, more important is the daily sustenance. "Drink your milk! Eat your vegetables! Finish your chicken." We know as parents it's our job to ensure that kids get all the daily requirements of minerals and vitamins they need to grow. We feed them that which promotes health and sustains them. However, what has often been the approach with catechesis? If anything, it tends to be superficial and artificial. *Sugary*. I know, I know . . . they're children. You don't give an infant steak or a toddler lobster risotto. But why is it that children's teaching is often the equivalent to a fruit rollup? Why is that we insist on watering down every teaching to the smallest component part? As if catechesis is a sugary snack?

Children have a robust capacity to ingest and soak up their environment through what they see and hear (and taste and smell). Whether they can articulate it or not, children from ages zero to seven retain a tremendous amount of content.[4] It is after third grade that they begin to ask more complex questions about "why" and "how." But children retain what they hear (Bible stories), see (liturgical colors and the symbols of the paraments), and imitate what they notice others doing around them (what they do) from a very early age. It's more caught than taught.

So, how do you "feed" a four year old word and sacrament? Teaching them to make the sign of the cross. This is a powerful reminder of their baptism (the connection you make for them) that is tactile and sensory. Teaching prayers and parts of the liturgy that they themselves can say in worship is also effective. One of the most formative things for children is to be brought to the communion rail. They see (up close!) the reception of the Sacrament. They smell the wine. They hear the words of the pastor. They even hear the crunch of the wafer. They receive a blessing from the pastor, who puts his hands on their head, hearing the words connecting them to their baptism. They can fold their hands during prayer. Standing up and sitting down when appropriate. All of these things collectively begin to imprint on your little one's soul, psyche, their hearts, hands, and minds. An even more radical notion, you might even sit up front with your kids so they can actually see what's going on!

This presumes that children are (a) being brought to worship, (b) intentionally and actively instructed and corrected while there, and (c) reinforcing these practices and rituals at home, in the car, on a walk. But let's talk about going to worship specifically in the life of catechesis. To be blunt—without regular attendance in worship, there can be no faith formation. This goes for *any person of any age*. It is such a simple premise that it's often overlooked. Worship is the beginning of it all, from the time we are born. This begins, not at some arbitrary age when a child is thought to be "accountable," but from the cradle. Does a child understand everything going on? No. Do you? Do I, for that matter? No. Comprehension is not the key, but total and regular immersion into the life of the church lived out in the body of Christ, week in, week out. Worship is also the "end" of catechesis, that is, the goal of it. We are trying to form a lifelong disciple of Christ. We are actively instructing one who is to continue to receive Christ's gifts of Word and Sacrament. Catechesis is not a test you pass. It is not a craft project. It is not a hoop to be jumped through. *Catechesis is lifelong*

---

4. This is also the concern with screens and all the ways that *PIL* can be delivered to children.

instruction into the life of faith, that they might grow and mature in Christ. The hope is that they will have children, and instruct them in the faith.

Let Them Experience Belonging (Stop the Segregation!)

But as we look throughout American Christianity, there is a fundamental difference of opinion and practice over children's role in worship. Some people want to *remove* them from worship, or offer "children's church" as an alternative. Children belong in worship, just as much as ninety-four-year-old Grandma Schmidt does. It's not about behaving (though they have to learn to), it is about *belonging*. Belonging is experienced through direct engagement in worship practices. From cradle to grave.

As stated above, children of a very young age can begin to participate in worship. They can fold their hands to pray. The can learn basic responses like "amen" and "also with you." They can sing parts of the liturgy. So, as early as possible we should train them to participate. Every child is different; not all children have the same attention spans. But there are certainly moments of engagement that any child can enter into to belong. Through active participation in worship, children feel like they belong, that they have a role, and that worship is a place for them to be, not be taken out of until they are older and understand better. This doesn't mean that this is easy! It means that it is intentional. Parents and grandparents have to model the behavior, actively teach and correct, and even put them in a position to see. Consistency is the key, and it doesn't happen overnight. The goal is that they begin to feel like they are part of something and not a visitor in "adult things."

Parents Make Better Choices and Have New/Different Priorities

The responsibility for lasting catechesis comes down to parents. The pastor has very little direct impact on children. The parents are the ones who make the difference.[5] More specifically, *the critical figure in long term catechesis is the father.* It is the head of the household who will make the most enduring impression. In one well-known study, it was shown that the highest percentage of children who stayed in the faith was in a household where the father sang in worship! Tragically, many fathers are not only absent from worship, but from the household. There are many broken families

---

5. This, by the way, is true of so many things!

into which others have to step up. I personally was raised in that situation. However, despite the breakdown of the family, the ideal model is not negated. The point is that a mother and father who (a) bring their children to worship every Sunday, (b) model the faith at home through prayer and intentional devotional time, and then (c) actively participate themselves in worship *do more to teach their children than any program, activity, or congregational event ever could.* It is, in fact, the way God designed humans to learn, through mom and dad, over time through repetition.

It comes down to parents making better choices. A family that eats together, prays together. A family that eats and prays together, worships together. But how often does the busyness of life . . . all the school activities, social events, sports, etc., get in the way of simply sitting down together to have a meal? If you have children at home (of any age), how many times a week are you eating a meal at the same time, at the same table (without a screen involved)? If it's less than five, then better decisions need to be made. If this seems like I am being intrusive, well, yeah! I'm a pastor! Pastors get into people's business. It's called spiritual instruction. I am attempting to catechize *you*! It's my job and calling. What you do with it is your choice.

Maybe you would like to make some changes, but are overwhelmed by where to start. Maybe you are doing some things suggested but don't see the possibility of doing more. The basic question we must all ask—*what is our priority for our family and children or grandchildren?* What is our greatest hope for them? Who do we want them to become? What do we want their heart to fix upon for a lifetime? If the answer to any of those questions is a lifelong active participant in the kingdom of God, *then tough choices have to be made.* Actions have to be taken, like, now. It's not too late, though; it's never too late. So, maybe you start small and simple. Try to eat dinner together two nights a week. Have a special family prayer time once a week. Invite dad to read the Bible at devotion. And maybe we can say "no" to doing everything everyone else does, and have better priorities.

A Catechesis That Lasts for a Lifetime

In the end, catechesis that lasts is predicated on boring consistency. Doing the same things over and over and over until it *bores* into hands and hearts and creates habits. It's not exciting. It often seems pointless. We must refrain from our sinful urge to make every single thing entertaining and instead seek the things that are edifying and grounded in the truth and beauty of God. So, it's day in, day out. It's even when you don't feel like it. What begins to happen, though, is that *God's Word and Spirit change hearts and minds*. He forms and shapes and molds and fashions. He gives us many ways to receive what he has to give. We are called to be willing recipients.

I write this because nearly everyone I interact with, even in my own congregation, is resistant to the above suggestions. Instead, the sentimental urge is always pulling at us to repristinate and retry everything that has *failed* us in the past. "If we do it better this time, then we'll get the kids, and the families." Catechesis that lasts is not about doing something innovative or exciting. It is actually getting back to how the church has taught for nearly two thousand years. Through instruction in the word, through worship, in the context of the family. I propose we go back, not to the past of the twentieth century, but to the core principles and approaches that make enduring disciples for life. It is this way that we will keep people in the church, by growing them into it, that they may be formed and shaped by Christ. This is why we start with catechesis. There really are no magic bullets to any of the big questions. However, the slow drip of *PIL* can be counteracted by the slow drip of lifelong and intentional catechesis.

A SECOND, LONGER *TECHNOLOGY* CONVERSATION—A TOOL USED FOR THE GOOD

I SPEAK NOW TO both individuals and parents who are in charge of the technology of the household. First, we must purge the "old leaven" out of our midst. This demands an honest and thorough assessment of how much *PIL* we daily engage in ourselves through various forms of technology. Where is it? Are there things we casually watch or listen to without thinking? *Be aware.* What kinds of things draw our heart away from Jesus? What is the technology situation of our households? Is there easy access to *PIL*? What about our children and grandchildren's access? *Be discerning.* Making an honest assessment, we then make better choices. While this can be manifested in many ways, I focus on the smart phone.

To condemn all technology as bad gets us nowhere, so we need to deal positively with the Christian quandary: how is a faithful Christian to rightly use God's gift of technology? To be specific to our topic, how do people navigate smart phones and the internet, especially if they are trying to prohibit engagement in *PIL*? Filters and secure web browsers are a start, but they are half measures at best. They can be easily gotten around by any third grader. We need to do better than automatically handing over technology to people who are not capable (through lack of maturity and formation) to handle it.[6] To make my case, I use an analogy.

The Saw

While I don't know anything about furniture building, I do like to watch YouTube videos of regular people who build intricate, beautiful pieces of

---

6. This includes many adults I know!

furniture.[7] You see people using the best slabs of wood, the best tools, taking care to be precise in all that they do. It's rewarding to see the process unfold to the finished product. I was watching a video the other day of a husband and wife team building an eight-foot dining room table from a live slab of black walnut. Preparing the raw material of wood to become a finished table took hours to achieve. Through time-lapse photography, one could observe the process in a matter of a half an hour. But still! All of the technical mastery and precision that is required! The builders not only had the expertise but the tools. Some are pretty basic—a sander, a tool for clearing out loose sediment, a planer. Other tools, however, were really quite, well, *dangerous*. Powerful table saws, scroll saws. Very sharp. One slip up and *bam*! No fingers, like, forever. And forever is a mighty long time.

The saw used to rip straight lines off the ends of this piece of black walnut was a Festool T8 75 track saw with a thirty-six-inch Festool track. The track kept the cut straight while the saw made very precise cuts. It takes practice to use such a tool. One would never hand over a powerful saw to a novice such as myself, with no training, and say, "Have at it!" In fact, humans from time immemorial have employed a basic, strategic process for handing down knowledge, especially when working with something dangerous. For there are two dangers in the misuse of a tool—*making an irreparable mistake to the product* or *an irreparable mistake to the person.*

Imagine a father wants to build a big dining room table. He has built many tables before, but now he wants to show his growing teenage son how to do it—the whole process. From selecting the wood, preparing it, cutting it, screwing/gluing it together, staining it, drying it. In this, he shows his son how to use a dangerous tool like a saw. How would he do it? "Here you go! Hope it turns out! Good luck!" No. That would be absurd. Instead, he would use the age old practice of:

> I do, you watch
> I do, you help
> I help, you do
> I watch, you do

It's so imminently practical that you intuitively recognize this process.[8] But it's necessary. Because when teaching someone to use a tool that can make

7. The irony that my analogy starts with my "watching something on YouTube" is not lost on me.

8. The first time I came across this process was listening to Katy Faust, the executive and director of Them Before Us, a children's rights organization. While I don't believe she

very precise cuts, both to the material and finger(!), we take care to model, train, and oversee before simply handing over something like a saw to a child or growing teen.

- So, as the father does, the son watches him carefully. The father explains what he's doing and the mistakes he's made in the past.

- The father does, but this time the son helps out. He starts to get a feel for it, but the father is still in charge.

- But then there is a bit of a role-reversal. In the next stage the son starts to do, with the father helping out where needed.

- Finally, the son is able to do (use the sharp and precise saw) on his own. The father is always there lending support if needed.[9]

The average age a child gets a smart phone is twelve years old. Twelve. "Child" is the operative word. Most often, the phone is given over with no training and little discernment. Oh sure, there's "rules" (no texting after nine; only an hour after school) . . . blah, blah, blah . . . we're not doing a good job of training our children with a dangerous piece of technology that has direct access to *PIL* and so much more. While I'm not prescribing an appropriate age for smartphones, it sure ain't twelve.

Brothers and sisters in Christ, a smart phone is not a neutral tool! It is a "saw" . . . a potential window into every manner of debauchery. It just is. Oh, it's a tool, but one carefully designed to illicit increasing usage by the user. It is a tool to draw people in. Into what? Another world.[10] Unlike other forms of technology (a paintbrush, for instance), smart phones and tablets are portals. Not like flipping through the pages of a magazine, it's like flipping through the pages of every magazine in every store in every country! This is one reason why pornography has exploded in the last fifteen years. Phones give people instant access to another universe. Very often, that universe is dark and dangerous. We must be vigilant when and how much we allow our children to use them without the proper training. Maybe *we should be a bit more intentional* with our own use of technology around our

---

is the innovator of this process, I credit her as the source of exposure for me.

9. It did enter my mind that another analogy might be one of a mother teaching her daughter to shave her legs. Seeing as how I am a father with two daughters, I thought I'd better stick with saws and sons!

10. I speak both of the hardware and software/algorithms used. Not neutral!

children. For they learn from what we're doing. So, we are to be prudent and model the behaviors we'd like to see from them.

Speaking more broadly, we are to be the gatekeeper. We are to protect our children from evil. Nothing comes to our children's eyes unless it gets through us. During my time at Barnes & Noble, I became very familiar with the children's and teen book sections. A lot of garbage! But I would meet parent after parent who would buy the child anything, with the rationalization, "As long as they're reading." No! Don't let them read things that are *not* truly excellent, *not* edifying, *not* glorifying God's truth and beauty. A gatekeeper both restricts and encourages. Encourage children to read excellent books. And there are excellent books out there. But "whatever" doesn't work. There are many books in the teen section of a bookstore that I would blush to read. Just because something is on a reading list doesn't mean it passes your gate. In fact, being the gatekeeper means that you have to read things first. That's right, you have to read as a parent. Nothing gets past your gate without your examination. Positively, this means you have a wonderful privilege to introduce your children and family to beauty. There are some great resources out there for books. There is great literature that the whole family can enjoy (again and again). But being gatekeeper also means that you can be the one to introduce beauty into the home, into the car, into the orbit of the child. Artwork that depicts biblical narrative in a realistic and imaginative way. Music that lifts and inspires. You can shape the standard and set the tone. But as gatekeeper, it also means that your standards have to be high.

High standards in gatekeeping must apply to social media and technology. This is hard for some. Do our children *have to be* on Facebook, Instagram, TikTok? And if so, what age? Do we even ask questions like, "What is an appropriate age to allow my child to be on social media?" If we ask, do we listen to the advice? I don't know . . . honestly, as a pastor, father, as someone who thinks and cares deeply about these issues, *I have never once been consulted on this question.* My observation is that most parents show little discernment, but instead permit, and then try to restrict. That way, they feel as if they're not depriving but still parenting. But part of parenting by its very definition is to restrict. Instead, many allow children access to social media, then try to govern it with guidelines. This seems problematic. Remember the analogy of the saw . . . "No sawing after nine! No sawing on a school night!" We have to train and monitor first, because once they have access, how do you limit their exposure? Perhaps we wait until they are fully matured adults before we allow our *children* to set up online accounts. Perhaps we should be better stewards of our children's online access and presence. For there are some very dangerous predators out there. I am not claiming to have the ironclad answers. I am claiming that we are not doing it well. We are not being discerning. With our own habits and our children's.

Technology for Good: Accountability Measures

The good news is that technology can be used for noble purposes. God is the creator of all things. Technology is a creation of God. Some things are used for honorable use, others . . . not so much. So, there are some measures that families can employ to protect themselves and loved ones from stumbling upon *PIL* and avoid temptation.

I am writing for a family context, but the suggestions below work for individuals as well. I by no means offer exhaustive research on what works best. There are too many factors to consider; finding what fits your situation takes time, research, and customization.[11] But there are several available avenues to block content and limit exposure to pornography.

Pornography Blocking Software, Filters, and Other Technology

There are dozens of pornography blocking software packages and systems available. Some are free, and others cost. The cost depends on how many devices and how extensive the blocking or limitation you desire. For instance, you can get a basic package for five devices and then pay more as you add on. Or you can get a basic filtering/blocking one, and then pay to block or limit social media platforms. What is it generally that these software packages can do?

- There are usually some kind of parental controls
- There is usually an internet filter
- There is usually a porn blocking feature
- There is usually some kind of screen time management feature

11. It is ironic—we must spend more time on the internet to find out ways to spend less time on it!

- There is usually some kind of time management tracking and reporting feature
- There is usually some specific app blocking feature
- There is usually some kind of location tracking feature

Several companies will do the above (or a combination at a price)—either for a monthly fee or a yearly amount.

Website Blockers, VPNs, and Partner-Based Accountability Apps

There are many basic technology tools that can aid in the control and flow of *PIL* into the household. Website blockers can be installed. Some are free (and then upgradable) and others cost. While not foolproof, most can limit things from popping up unexpectedly. Most blockers won't provide tracking and data on usage, however. VPNs, or virtual private networks, are mini-networks that run through your internet connection. They give you a fair amount of control over everything you (and your family) watch, and usually cost around one hundred dollars a year. The next level of pornography blocking is apps that provide an alert system to a partner or "ally." This enables another person to be informed when lines are crossed. One such company is Covenant Eyes, a Christian-based program that provides not only blocking software but offers training in accountability measures. If you are a person struggling with pornography addiction/compulsion, this type of system is the best way to help with going onto sites. Allies can be utilized to help with temptation and walking back from crossing a boundary. These systems are not fool proof, but give a good line of defense. These types of packages will run around 150 to 180 dollars a year.

The Bottom Line

All of the above can be used as tools to help manage internet usage. They can protect individuals and the family from encountering unwelcome intrusions into your home. There is an old saying in Alcoholics Anonymous—if you don't want a haircut, don't hang out in a barber shop. While completely staying off the internet may not be feasible, if you don't want to be tempted or have your family exposed, then this technology is necessary. However, technology restrictors in no way take the place of good parenting practices. There are no foolproof methods. All technology can be gotten around by a savvy internet user. These are simply a good first line of defense. It is like installing a security system in your house—it gives a measure of protection and some peace of mind. But it can also give people a false sense of security. The technology cannot take the place of side-by-side parenting, friendship, and pastoral care.

A Home Life of Relationships Instead of Screens

Positively, while implementing filtering and blocking technology (that good solid mortar lock on the front door), the most important thing is that a home is *filled with beauty*. It should be a place of conversation. A beautiful home limits access to technology. It promotes and inculcates face-to-face, in-person relationships and interactions. *Face to face.* Starting at home, we have spaces (say the dinner table) where any form of technology is forbidden. Instead, activities and interactions are done by looking at another human being (whom you presumably love). No screens in sight, no ballgame on in the background. Whether it's playing cards or games or just (gasp) talking to one another, this simple fix is powerful. We have to reclaim the ability to have in-person conversations and spend time together. We must aspire to the beautiful home.

Does this mean no family movie night? Does this mean no Spotify playing through the speaker system? Does this mean no internet in the home? Does this mean you give up all technology? No . . . but it does mean that we don't fight technology with technology. Instead *we create common family spaces*. Places in the home where everyone can gather. We limit our screens to just a few visible places in the house. No bedrooms! It means that phones are put away when the family is gathered. We are conscious about our time together. Let's give our technology a sabbatical.

One of my favorite things to do is listen to podcasts. It is one of the ways I did research for writing this book. But the wireless headphone innovation is my personal trap. Because I can be at home with my family and be completely absorbed into my own world. "Did Daddy hear us or did he have his ear buds in?" Personal changes in habit are necessary for all of us. But we must treasure the home life and the time God gives us to spend together. Modeling this for our children is powerful. They will do what they see us do, if not sooner, definitely later! We must make our homes places for quality time together, building relationships, and fellowship. It sounds so easy, doesn't it? But it is hard to do. It must be an intentional goal and lifestyle.

We can also encourage our children to develop friendships with other children who share our same goals and values. This sounds hopelessly old-fashioned, and I realize that children are around other children all day in school . . . but what about encouraging good old "play dates" and family interactions over common interests? I am specifically talking to those in the church. Do we seek out *other church families* for our children to learn to be sociable with and around? I recently heard of a group of families that get together every year to watch the movie *The Princess Bride* and drink root beer. Could it be this simple, a movie and a beverage?

Creating opportunities to interact and socialize with people who share your world view is just one way to protect our children and promote friendship and community. Technology cannot be the replacement for every single thing. It can do a lot of tasks, but it does a poor job of keeping us connected. In fact, the research suggests it actually drives us apart! So, we must be intentional about forming friends and social groups so that our children learn how to appropriately interact with each other. Eventually, this approach might be how people find a suitable spouse . . .

Excursus
Self-Control

But before the dating conversation, we pause to talk about another unmentionable. *Self-control.* In a world where everything is on demand; where a twenty-four-hour store is always open; where we can get literally anything we want delivered to our homes, what place does self-control have any more in our lives? "You mean I have to 'wait' for something and steward my instincts/desires while I wait?" Yes.

We might start with what self-control is. *It is a fruit of the Spirit.* It is a restraint of impulse and emotion. It was seen to be a virtue by the Greek philosophers.[1] It was even something that Paul argued before the Roman procurator.

> After some days Felix came with his wife Drusilla, who was Jewish, and he sent for Paul and heard him speak about faith in Christ Jesus. And as he reasoned about righteousness and *self-control* and the coming judgment, Felix was alarmed and said, "Go away for the present. When I get an opportunity I will summon you."[2]

Righteousness, the coming judgment, and *self-control.* A very strange triad! Must have been a wide-sweeping sermon. Whatever the exact context, Luke wants the reader to know that it was among the topics Paul felt important enough to present in a defense of the gospel and faith in Christ Jesus.

But our problem with self-control is not merely our lack of understanding or definition. *Our problem is in our lack of practice.* As mentioned, self-control doesn't fit within our modern lifestyle. We are never asked to show any; indeed we are not even trained in it. If anything, we

1. They seemed to be a bit obsessed about self-control!
2. Acts 24:24–25.

might be implored to "practice patience" (like a child waiting a few hours to open a Christmas gift), but we are never required to show anything like *restraint*. Perhaps self-control should reenter the Christian lexicon and actually be taught.

For (I say again) it is a fruit of the Spirit of Christ. In other words, this is something manifested in believers. Self-control (also known as temperance) is seen *against a world of excesses*. It is a controlling of both the flesh and the will. Restraint against fornication, restraint against gluttony, restraint against general revelry. Self-control, though, is not simply "mind over matter." It is about changing the aim of the heart that then directs your body toward other pursuits. A lot of what I recommend earlier in part 3 is finding ways to redirect both heart and hands, mind and body away from the "desires of the flesh." This is the phenomenological way we experience the Spirit's fruit. The re-creational way of the "fulfilling the law of Christ."

A more mundane way people speak of self-control (the Greek *en-krateia*) is of moderation.[3] But perhaps it's better to speak of temperance (Greek *sophrosune*), which is a higher rank above moderation. Temperance is a kissing cousin to self-control. It is one of the "four hinges that swing the gate of life."[4] Temperance (also known as sobriety) is what St. Paul says that man and woman must continue in for salvation—faith, love, holiness, with temperance.[5] With respect to chastity, self-control flows from an ordered self, one who is in control of impulses and sees the truth objectively. The temperate person, one governed by self-control, practices restraint over himself and his own needs, to promote the good of others. The person *lacking* in self-control is one who gives into impulses, but not for the good. An absence of self-control is the abandonment of prudence and the embodiment of the "self-will run riot."

As we turn to dating, courtship, and finding a mate (and all that that entails), if the two people engaged in the noble pursuit of marriage are not practicing self-control, then dating leads into self-centered endeavors of debauchery. We must be sober in what steps we take. There is also a reason this topic is in the "family" section—self-control must be inculcated by the mother and father. This fruit of the Spirit lives in the household of ones who are dead to sin and alive to God in Christ Jesus. This is part of catechesis. If

---

3. I hesitate using this term though, because moderation gets misconstrued as a problem with mere quantity. As we have discussed, pornography *in any amount* is a problem!

4. Pieper, *Four Cardinal Virtues*, 145.

5. 1 Tim 2:15.

one cannot practice self-control, then one is not ready to date . . . no matter the age of the child or adult.

A *DATING* CONVERSATION FOR THE CHRISTIAN—
TOWARD THE GOOD OF MARRIAGE

WHY THIS TOPIC IN a book about *PIL* and pornography? Because it's not enough to condemn behavior, calling it out and diagnosing the problem. I also seek to offer an alternate view of the universe to the one given by the culture. Since there is a distinction between the Christian and secular worldview, there should also be a distinction between the way we conduct our lives. But very often, Christian practices look exactly the same as the world's! Nothing exemplifies this more than dating.[6] Pornography has warped the collective brain of America and changed how people view the opposite sex, *but also how people practice (or don't practice) dating.* I offer something for families, for parents and their children to follow that is different than the world. Instead of trying to sanitize the world's practice of dating, perhaps we should return to something more rooted in God's will for those in Christ.

I realize that I am writing to people who might be in different seasons of life. Maybe you are a lifelong bachelor. Perhaps a widow or widower. You might be a grandparent. Maybe an older single who hasn't found the right person yet. You might be someone who is happily married and did everything differently from what I propose. But we all want what's best, not just for our families, but for the saints in the church. So, this topic is important for families, *but also for you* because as Christians we all have roles to play in the habits and practices of dating and marriage. No one gets to sit this play out.

---

6. When I use the term "dating," I am referring to the modern dating rituals and practices commonly seen between most grade and high school children, extending into adulthood.

Part Three: The "Cure" for the Self, the Family, and the Congregation

The dating discussion that follows is organized under the headings of three axioms[7]—"Love Is Obedience," "Boys Lie and Girls Manipulate," and "Dating Is for Married People." After the initial discussion, using both a biblical and secular narrative, I propose a way to try to navigate this issue with our own children, raising some questions and suggesting some practices.

First Things in the Dating Conversation

Before we begin, however, we must place this discussion within the framework of God's will for his redeemed and renewed creatures with respect to human sexuality. For as you might guess, I am hunting bigger game than simply dating. For the issues abound. One is that *a number of young people don't even date*. Are they interacting with the opposite sex? Many, yes. Are they doing so in a chaste and God-pleasing way? Certainly not. The usage of dating apps, which are used to hook up, has greatly altered the interaction between the sexes. All of this, driven by the rampant promiscuity signaled in our culture, has led many Christians to delay marriage or not seek marriage at all. As for having children, many are waiting to have kids or even opting not to.

There are also conversations concerning key topics people need to have early on in the process. Unfortunately, they're kicked down the road until a dating couple has spent significant time together, even *after* they get married. But conversations centered on shared goals and values are crucial. We can break them down into four categories:

- Faith—are both from the same faith tradition? Do both worship Christ?

- Finances—what is the view of money and debt? Keep a budget or run up credit cards?

- Children—what is the hope and desire for having children? Do both even want kids?

- Extended Family—are there members of the family that are hard to deal with? Is the potential mother-in-law eccentric or domineering?

7. Again, I give full credit to Pastor Scott Bruzek as one of the inspirations of this rethinking.

If people had these conversations *after the first couple of dates*, then better decisions would be made with respect to finding a lifelong spouse. Divorces would also go down because these are the things that drive people to end a marriage. So, as I talk about the topic of dating, please remember that there are underlying issues afoot. But I also realize that amidst all that surrounds dating, we never seem to get around to actually talk about dating properly understood in the context of marriage and what God desires. With that said, let's begin our conversation.

Axiom #1: Love Is Obedience

The world has defined "love" entirely wrong. And if we get love wrong, *then our goals and actions looking for love will be wrongheaded*. So, here it is: love is not (primarily) an emotion. Do we feel things toward people? Yes. Do we "fall in love" with our potential spouses? Sure. But love seen through a biblical and Christological lens is about *service and sacrifice*. Love is obediently serving the needs of another and putting those needs above our own. It is the giving up of yourself for another. "Therefore be imitators of God, as beloved children. And walk in love, *as Christ loved us and gave himself up for us*, a fragrant offering and sacrifice to God."[8]

So, love is not a feeling but an action. It is busy, kind, and patient. It does not boast or draw attention to itself. When talking about dating, the goal is not to fall in love but to find a mate whom you will serve and give yourself to. So, if we put our wants, needs, and desires aside and instead are obedient to another's well-being, *we love that person*. Seeing love this way enables us to situate human relationships as imitators of God's love of us in his Son Jesus. Is there room in the love discussion for attraction and compatibility? Of course! That's a huge part of it. We naturally seek to marry someone whom we are attracted to and with whom we fit well, including values (see above). But as any married couple knows, there are seasons when the attraction is more muted. There are hard times that interfere with "the feelings." So, if love is based solely on some kind of inner, subjective feeling, we might be led to believe that "we're not in love anymore" when that feeling ebbs and flows.

8. Eph 5:1–2 (my emphasis).

Axiom #2: Boys Lie and Girls Manipulate

Now we are getting down to it! When talking to an audience of ladies, I emphasize the former (boys lie), but I realize that that might not be helpful if, say, some of them have sons! The point is: we must be brutally honest about the common interactions between the sexes, especially during the teen years. Boys of a certain age have only one thing on their mind; they will do and say anything to achieve their goals, especially in today's society. In fact, their peer groups will encourage this. Also, I know this because I was a boy once and am still a sinner! My basic point—*a girl should not believe anything that comes out of a boy's mouth until verified, double-checked, and co-signed by a third party.*

It's been pointed out to me that girls also lie. Duly noted. The broader claim being made is that both sexes operate with general but different patterns of sinful behavior. We've discussed boys. The pattern for girls is *to manipulate the single-mindedness of boys*. To play on their libido and turn their lust to their own end. Girls can play one boy off another with a look, a smile, a toss of the head. We all know this; it's not popular to say it. To give an example, I appeal to a well-known movie of the late sixties, *The Jungle Book*. At the end of the movie Mowgli and Baloo have defeated Shere Khan. It's time for Mowgli to return to the man-village. He doesn't want to go, until he meets a beautiful young village girl at the riverside. With a coquettish smile and a bat of the eyes, she "accidentally" drops her water jar so that Mowgli might fetch it and carry it for her. Spoiler alert—Mowgli is manipulated into going with her into town!

We must be honest about the sinful proclivities, manifested in each sex, especially as they relate to dating. Young people lack maturity, don't have the practice of enduring temptation, and are driven by unchecked hormones and urges. So, what do we commonly allow our children to do? Following the practice of the world, Christians let their children go on dates, spending time alone together *without any supervision and accountability.* We then act surprised when they fall into temptation and give full reign to their lust. Knowing what seems self-evident, we instead should rethink any modern dating practices for teens and even college-age kids. Is there an alternative?

Axiom #3: Dating Should Lead to Marriage and Is (Really) for Married People

If you're tracking with me, you see I am suggesting that we stop thinking of "dating" as an acceptable way for boys and girls to interact. That's because dating is for people who are already married. "Now you've lost your mind!" No, my mind is intact. I have thought through our common practices and where they inevitably lead. Let us start with the basic question—what is the purpose of dating? This leads to another basic principle—*dating must lead to marriage*. Let me put it this way. If dating is not meant to lead to marriage, then what is the purpose in letting our children date, sometimes as young as sixth grade? What is the goal? To practice? What is to be gained by allowing your daughter to go to a movie unchaperoned with a boy? What will happen if two eighth graders go off with a group of friends for a day trip to Six Flags (even if it's sanctioned by the local church youth group)?

I remember the first time I heard this challenge to dating. My knee-jerk reaction was to push back. I was married at the time, didn't have children, and had made many of the mistakes outlined above. I now realize my core objection was, "Surely *everyone* can't be wrong about this?" But the discussion stuck with me, because as I have said, most every *other* outcome in dating scenarios is rooted in sin. Think of how many times you've heard well-meaning Christians say things like, "I just want my kids to have fun in college and date around" or "They're too young to settle down; just date until you meet the right person." What do we give up, all in the name of making sure our children are "well-adjusted" and "socialized"?

So, my argument is: once you're married, then you date. That is, you spend time alone together, you share intimacy, you exchange romantic gestures. You have date nights. That's the fruit of marriage—*a lifelong, physical bond in which man and woman share a robust life together including intimacy.* But if you are "dating" before being joined together as one flesh, you will be tempted to engage in activities God reserves solely for marriage. Even an innocent dinner and a movie can tempt us to engage in practices that are not God pleasing. I certainly realize the need to get to know one another. But perhaps our engagements should be shorter and the implicit goal kept in view. Because casually dating has no place in the life of a Christian.

Stop right now and assess. If you accept that I might be right (even partially), then the big question is: how are boys and girls to meet someone and find a suitable mate to marry?

What Might Christian Dating Look Like? Two Stories

To illustrate my point biblically, I share the story of Isaac and his eventual wife Rebekah.[9] When Abraham was old in years, he sought a wife for his son Isaac. It was imperative that Isaac did not marry a woman from the land of Canaan (full of pagan idolatry), but one from his own tribe and family.[10] So, Abraham sent his most-trusted servant to the Mesopotamian city of Nahor. He was to take many choice gifts to honor the family and entice them to give a wife for Isaac. The angel of the Lord led this enterprise, ensuring that all would be done in accordance with God's will. So the servant went, and in a fortuitous encounter at the town well, he met Rebekah, a young woman very attractive in appearance and one who had been kept from men. *It was revealed that she was the one for Isaac.* Rebekah ran back and told her family she had met a servant of Abraham, and they invited him to dinner. They learned the purpose of his journey. He put a proposal to them for Rebekah's hand, couched in the free invitation from Abraham for his son Isaac. Rebekah's family was to choose whether they might accept the invitation for marriage or not. While the family accepted on her behalf, it was *Rebekah's choice whether she went immediately or remained for some days,* showing some autonomy and respect for her wishes. Rebekah and her women rose and went with Abraham's servant and his men. Isaac (not heard from in the story!) was dwelling in the Negeb, meditating in the fields. He lifted up his eyes and saw the caravan coming. Rebekah lifted up her eyes and saw Isaac. When she learned who it was, she covered herself with her veil. The servant told Isaac all that had transpired. Then Isaac brought Rebekah into the tent of Sarah his mother and took her for his wife. Consider that Isaac and Rebekah didn't "date," but *were joined together by a third party with their best interests at heart.* Also consider that Moses tells us explicitly that *Isaac loved Rebekah.*

To make my point even more provocatively, I reference a well-known story from the early seventies. It came to pass that a young man from New York was spending time with relatives in Sicily. One day while out for a walk, he came upon a young woman and was struck by her beauty, like a thunderbolt. Afterwards, in a near-by village, his companions related this experience to a local man. It soon became clear to the man that the

---

9. Gen 24:1–67.

10. That seems weird. We are talking extended family. Think of this more in terms of sharing the same worldview and value system.

young maiden they were describing *was his daughter*. He took great offense and became indignant. However, the young man spoke to him kindly and showed respect. He asked the father for permission to court his daughter with the intent of marriage. A meeting was arranged, in the company of the young girl's family. The man from New York brought gifts for the girl as well as her household. And so it was, *he was allowed to date her in the presence of her family*. In a poignant scene, the two are permitted *to walk alone together ahead of the party to share in some strictly supervised intimate conversation*. The family dined and the couple spent more time together, again in full view of all. They were finally married before the Lord and the whole village. It is then, *and only then*, that they are completely alone and intimate as husband and wife.

I imagine your reaction is incredulity. "Arranged marriages? Servants acting as go-betweens? Dowries given to the bride's family? This is twenty-first century America, Pastor Heaton!" That's right. This is the twenty-first century, and our dating practices, even within the fellowship of the church, resemble something more akin to a pagan, hedonistic, libertine sub-culture than what is appropriate in the body of Christ. Am I saying we should return to arranged marriages? Not exactly. Am I saying we should treat young women as property to be exchanged for goods and wealth? *Of course not.* Am I saying we should question the practice of letting a girl go on a date unchaperoned in the company of a boy? Well . . .

Both stories show significant cultural norms of their time that dictate the actions leading to matrimony. But both also have significant principles and behaviors grounded in and derived from God's natural Law. The starting point for a relationship was not a casual thing. It was undertaken with ceremony and serious protocol with the goal of matrimony in mind. At every turn, *the conversation and practices took place in the presence of the family*, or at least with the explicit sanction and permission of the family. What it was *not* was a more familiar scene. College kids Isaac and Rebekah jet in on Christmas break, announcing to the family that "they are getting married" and "want a big wedding" and "they are so excited!" Instead, seen in the second story, *there should be a progressing toward supervised freedom.* As with Isaac, there should be a conversation about what had been settled, while Rebekah was modestly veiled until the acceptable time. All was done openly with the consent of the prospective bridegroom and bride. What there was *not* was secrecy, passion, or "test drives." In all things, there was modesty, dignity, and decorum. Isn't that something that should interest sons and daughters of the King?

Where Does the Church Go from Here?

One of the biggest pushbacks I get is the very practical, "Where are you supposed to meet girls? Where are you gonna meet boys if you can't date?" I dunno . . . maybe the church! Shouldn't the church be more proactive about giving people of marriageable age venues and opportunities to mix and get to know potential spouses? Shouldn't families "socially engineer" (not marriages but) potential matches? Shouldn't local congregations use married lady members as "matchmakers"? Shouldn't families be involved in every step of the dating/courtship process, even when kids are away from home at college?

A final story, one that illustrates a different view of dating, told by the father of podcaster Allie Beth Stuckey. When Allie Beth (née Simmons) was in high school and began to date, her dad was determined he would meet *any* boy that wanted to take her out. They would have to come over beforehand and meet in his office (mortifying Allie Beth!). He would make prospective suitors sit on the other side of his desk in a chair (comically) a little shorter than his own. He would then question the young man. "I'm glad you're taking Allie Beth out tonight. What are you'll gonna do?" He would lay out ground rules about when to be home and "inappropriate touching." He would then pop the question: *Are you gonna marry my daughter?* The boy would be horrified. "No Mr. Simmons!" he would stammer. Her dad would reply, "Yeah, that's good. I didn't think so. I don't expect that. But you know what this means—it means that you are dating somebody else's wife tonight. It also means that someone is dating your wife. And I want you to treat Allie Beth the way you want your future wife treated. Can we do that?"[11] With respect to living in accordance with God's will, can we do that?

11. Stuckey and Simmons, "Allie's Dad on the Economy," 1:09:13.

PARENTING AS A PRE-MODERN: INCULCATING THE GOOD IN AN AGE OF *PIL*

WE PROTECT OUR FAMILIES in many other ways as well. We first model the behavior we want. For they'll do what we do. We center our lives (including our home life!) around Jesus. We practice forgiveness. Let them see it! We also stay informed of the threats and challenges (the entire purpose of this project) and plan strategic responses. We protect our children by having age-appropriate conversations at *every stage of life*. We respect their innocence by not flaunting the world at them. We recognize that little eyes and ears aren't ready for everything all at once. Some things should be "unmentionable"! But the flip side is, if we aren't the first ones to instruct and guide, *then we may as well be last*.[12] So, we monitor everything and act accordingly. We train, and pray, and study, and worship, and talk, and repeat. This is the way we protect our children, our families, ourselves. We start with Jesus and end with Jesus. Christ is all, and in all. And we use what he has given us—sanctified wisdom—to do what we are supposed to do.

In other words, we become a pre-modern parent.

Pre-Modern Parenting

What does is it mean to be a "pre-modern parent"? Is this a return to a proto-technological age? Do we disavow anything "modern"? Do we throw out our TVs and get rid of our smart phones? First things first. By premodern, *I mean that we do not measure our family life by any standards of the modern/contemporary age*. We are not holding ourselves up to anything other than what is good, true, and beautiful. That's our standard—God and

---

12. Your child will view the person they hear from *first* on a topic as the expert of that topic.

his design and everything that entails. We are not concerned with trends (though we employ what is helpful). We are not concerned with what others think about us (though we listen to others in our congregational sphere). We are not seeking the approval from anyone other than Christ and his church. We strive to adopt the posture of *I couldn't care less about "what it makes us look like."* This is all easily said. But done with great difficulty.

We are to be pre-modern and not post-modern. For all the ways that term gets used, for my purposes, *post-modernity is a complete rejection of objective truth, morality, and convention.* It is true we live in a post-modern, post-Christian society. We need to understand how to operate within it, but we do not parent in a vacuum of morality. Quite the opposite. We actually consider a time before. Before smart homes; before every conceivable want and need was tracked by apps; before every purchase was data-mined by brokers of such things. We parent in a *timeless way* according to timeless truths rooted in God's will. For there are enduring, irrefutable, standards derived from God's natural Law. What does this look like?

A home adorned with beauty and an absence of distractions. A home with quiet places and quiet time. A home with abundant play. Imaginative play. Play without screens. A home where nature intrudes, filled with constant reminders of God's good creation. A home with gardens and plants. A home filled with music. Not endlessly cacophonous, guttural, crunchy, abrasive noises, but music that is melodic, rhythmic, dynamic, beautiful, and ascendent. A home where any kind of screen time is carefully managed and scrupulously limited. *For everyone.* A home where most meals are eaten at a table facing your family. A home where bread is baked. A home where bees are kept and honey is harvested. A home where mom and dad are present. *Present.* Without headphones or earbuds. A home where there is chatter and conversation. A home where there is laughter. A home where fairy tales are told. Where books are read out loud, and great books re-read again and again. Where naps are had on Sunday. A home where things are built, repaired, and reused if possible. Where children draw, laugh, and run.

Yes, run. For a pre-modern home is one where children play *outside.* A lot. Where field trips are taken . . . not for school, but for genuine learning. Where trees are climbed. Where creeks are "creeked." Where parks are explored and trails traversed. Where families walk and talk and breathe the fresh air. Where birds are identified. Where nature is explored and delighted in. Where neighbors are known and greeted. Where church is ideally right down the street.[13] Maybe this portrait aggravates you because you see it as an impossibility. Hopelessly idealistic. But shouldn't we aspire to something more, something better? Isn't "settling" what has gotten us in the *PIL* predicament we're in?

Maybe it's helpful to talk about what the pre-modern home *is not*. A pre-modern parent and home is one not *focused solely on the self.* For that is always *PIL's* aim—to make the self the center of every single thing. But the very root of sin is to be "curved in on oneself." To naval gaze. The founding of our great country, which has given us so many blessings from our Creator, is based on Enlightenment ideals. While we prize the endowed creaturely rights given by God and protected by our founding documents, the individual self is not the center of the universe. God is the center of life and the center of the home. The individual is completely "given to" by the Creator. So what has happened over the last two centuries? We've turned the ideals of our constitution into some sort of "me" project. We call them "rights," but ones disconnected from what is given and turned into stuff we want. Because we as sinners are always focused on our own desires. We crave "me time" and felt-needs met at every turn. But at what cost? What has the service of the self gotten our families?

This is starting to get philosophical. "I thought this section was to be practical!" Turns out the concrete needs the transcendent to aspire to and copy. Again, I write to Christians, the redeemed in Christ, who want something better for our families. At some point, we must assess how we're doing, then try to do better. A project of the pre-modern parent is to improve what we've been given in order to improve our stewardship of it. *It is a never-ending project.* The pre-modern home both rejects some things *and* inculcates others. Within this project, there is so much variety in God's good creation. A lot of space for preference and taste and inclination. But what we do resist is the "choice-at-all-cost" lifestyle. For the way of the modern (and post-modern) home is *slavery to choice.* To choosing all the wrong things. Things rooted and grounded in *PIL.* So, the pre-modern parent makes choices, sometimes endlessly it seems, *but ones that prioritize the family and how their home life is preserved.* This gives us terrific freedom using God's good gifts he provides and the boundaries he sets. But this type of parenting requires both a mom and dad to play their parts.

---

13. Much of this stream of consciousness flows from a terrific book by Esolen, *Ten Ways to Destroy the Imagination of Your Child.* The title as well as the book is ironic.

Part Three: The "Cure" for the Self, the Family, and the Congregation

A Word for Fathers

Fathers, you have a tough job. You are supposed to be many things—the breadwinner, the hero, the protector, the one who gives up selfish pursuits for your family. You are supposed to be so much. But we always fall short. According to our sinful nature inherited from our first father, we retreat. We are supposed to be on the front lines, taking charge, bearing responsibility. Instead we sit back. We escape. We might even struggle with the very issue I am discussing. So, we need models to copy. Many fathers of this age come from fatherless homes. So many fathers-to-be have no one spurring them on and encouraging them to embrace their role to come. The deck is stacked against you. Your own sinful flesh is constantly telling you to withdraw, your sinful wife is on your case, like all the time(!), and you just want to be left alone.

But your families need you. Your wife needs you. Without you, the whole thing falls apart. We are witnessing this on a massive societal scale. We know the costs if we fail. But I write to encourage you—to actually instill courage in your heart. God has created you for a purpose. He has designed a role for you to play. Wherever you are in your faith walk or personal piety, the call is made. Repent of your sins, receive the mercy of Christ, and get into the fray. Your wife needs you to lead. By the power of God and the Spirit of Jesus, you can do it.

A Word for Mothers

Mothers, you have a tough job. For the first, like, eighteen years of your child's life, they need you. Many times only you will do. Even for sons. "Mama" is the first word uttered and continues to be a frequent call through the child's existence. "Mom! Mother! Mama! I need you!" So, you are put upon and depended upon for so much from the jump. You're the one who is going to nurse that baby. You're the one called on to quiet that screaming infant. Every piece of clothing you own is stained with spit-up. As much as your husband tries to help, you really wish he wouldn't. "He'll just screw it up!" For you have inherited the sin of the first mother. Your desire is even against your husband. But he shall rule over you. An impossible situation. "How can he rule when I can't get him to show up!" You are frustrated. There's never enough time, mainly for yourself. You are always last. Every day is "father's day" but Mother's Day comes once a year, and even then you still are on duty.

But your families need you. Your husband needs you. Without you, the whole thing falls apart. You are the heart of the family. You are the natural voice of encouragement. You are the queen of the home. You are on the front lines, daily, no matter your career or vocation, for you still are "mama." You are the prayer warrior. Your families need your prayers, even after they have left the nest. But I write to encourage you, for the encourager needs encouragement! God has created you for a purpose. He has given you unique and special gifts. He has designed a role for you to play. Wherever you are in your faith walk or personal piety, the call is made. Repent of your sins, receive the mercy of Christ, and get into the fray. Your husband needs you now. He needs your strength and your support. By the power of God and the Spirit of Jesus, you can do it.

Chapter Fourteen

Congregational Conversations to Combat *PIL*

I HAVE TALKED ABOUT the single sinner trapped in a lifestyle of *PIL*. I've talked about households and families trying to navigate our present challenges. But congregations also need to take action. The first step is awareness, the stated purpose of this book. We need to know the gravity of the problem and how corrosive it truly is. This means being students of the word and students of God's good creational order and design.

First and foremost, the church is to proclaim the gospel. It is to announce the free forgiveness of Jesus for all people all the time. It is the church's *raison d'être*. Thankfully, I believe many congregations do this. That's been my experience in my home denomination, the LCMS. And we must keep doing this. The gospel is to be the center of what the church does. However. We have been assaulted the last several decades by views antithetical to God's natural Law. God's Law is available to all people, written on the heart of every man. God's Law, simply put, is *his will for his creation*. We need to embrace what God *actually* teaches us in his book of nature, the study of science and biology.[1] We need to be discerning about how the world is supposed to work according to God's design. This is also corroborated and articulated in Scripture. Man and woman functioning

---

1. Science is not opposed to God but the is study of his creation.

according to God's good plan has a tremendous effect to counteract all of the wickedness we see, ideas we have been lapping up through the entertainment industry for decades. Part of fighting back is to be grounded in the truth. To acknowledge there is truth and that God is the arbiter and purveyor of it. This means studying, reading, and seeking outside help to put it all together. There are tremendous resources available. *The church needs to make them available and encourage their usage.*

The church also has to do a better job of catechizing our children, teens, parents, and everyone in between. We need to preach regularly against *PIL*, and conduct robust Bible classes and workshops.[2] Christian publishing houses must make more resources available on a wide variety of topics relating to *PIL*. Let's instead use technology for good, truth, and beauty. It is a tool and can be an effective weapon in the fight. There are many other ways the church can fight too. Singles should be encouraged to marry and *taught* to be chaste while waiting. Perhaps the local congregation can be an appropriate place for men and women to meet and socialize.[3] Married couples should be encouraged to start families. Fathers and mothers need to be prayed for, mentored, and also held accountable. Recognize their job is not easy! We should celebrate them, but also come alongside and give them help. *It is a scary time to raise children.* The church should be right there, in Word and Sacrament ministry, but also providing some of the real human needs for our people. Churches can support women who are single parents through gifts and assistance. Congregations can host men's Bible studies to mentor younger men in faithful masculinity. The church can be a place of reconciliation and healing for those broken by addiction and compulsive viewing of pornography. All of this is part of the "how" we can fight against Satan and his designs. Being the church in every way, in every place, for every person.[4] In a phrase, the church is to be the church. Nosing into the lives of our people and communities. Involved. Curious. Ready to help. Compassionate.

I am speaking in generalities, so let me be more concrete. It's one thing to say, "encourage marriage" and "start families." It's another thing to make this "live" in the congregation. So, to combat *PIL*, and to also promote what

2. One example is to model for parents conversations on technology limitations in the home.

3. This is explored more below.

4. This truly is the vision of Paul—the vertical reality of God's people receiving his grace and mercy in Jesus Christ alone, and the horizontal reality of how we love our neighbor through active service.

is good and God pleasing, congregations have to, so to speak, get their hands dirty. We have to be intentional. To actually make a cultural change within our congregations, we need to help those eligible and inclined to marry *do just that*. I realize that marriage and families are not the answer to every single problem. But strengthening them is the place to start. Take a step back and consider. Pornography is rooted in sin and perversion, lust and licentiousness. To pull out the roots, to make a change in behaviors, starts with families. Every single ill that we see in society can either be fixed or aided by stronger families. *This is no different for pornography.* The people who are in the business of pornography don't generally come from two-parent families that are teaching the faith at home. That live and model the forgiveness of Jesus. They come from broken families, filled with abuse and addiction. They come from loss and isolation. So, never losing our reason for being, disciple-making proclaimers of the gospel, congregations must be a place that nurtures and strengthens family formation and sustenance.

Below are three approaches that can be done at the congregational level able to be customized to fit different sizes and contexts. They can be accomplished through smaller parishes getting together and sharing resources. But, principally, these are things that involve the people of God, the life of the church, with a practical eye to the future.

A WORD ON BEING SINGLE

To the unmarried and the widows I say that it is good for them to remain single, as I am. But if they cannot exercise self-control, they should marry. For it is better to marry than to burn with passion.

—1 Cor 7:8–9

But before I make my recommendations . . . some may question what I've said about dating and will be even more put off by what I'm getting ready to say. So let me be clear—being single is also a godly vocation and there are many faithful single Christian men and women. *Being single is not a sin.* St. Paul was an unmarried man! He had some very pointed things to say about that vocation![5] Being a "single" in the body of Christ does not make you somehow incomplete or less than whole. Please do not hear me say this. Some faithful Christians are single by choice, others by circumstance,

---

5. 1 Cor 7:25–40.

others by possessing the gift of chaste celibacy.[6] *My promotion of marriage and families is not an attack on singles.* I understand, though, that it might feel that way, especially when people like myself "go on and on about getting married."[7] I'm not attempting to alienate people who are not married. In talking to singles, I also understand they do feel pressure, or even feel ostracized by not being married (especially after a certain age). It's a real thing. We should pray for those who desire a spouse but have not found one, for those who are lonely, and pray that singles live faithfully in their vocation. Just know that what I say below is not meant to cause offense, but to address the issue of solitary men and solitary women doing their own thing, delaying marriage and having children because they want to "live their best life now." It is to *encourage people to marry if they are dating* and *encourage congregations to be places of assistance in this endeavor.* While being married may not be for everybody, *burning with lust in the single existence is not God's desire.* If the sin of lust is an ongoing issue, then perhaps being single is not the best vocation for you. "But because of the temptation to *porneia*, each man should have his own wife and each woman her own husband."[8]

Congregations must seek to enfold singles into their social life, just as they must enfold all ages. The diversity we see on Sunday morning in worship should be reflected in the what we do together outside worship. All too often we segregate and go off into groups. While there is nothing wrong with "singles groups" or "couples clubs," there is a kink in our koinonia if that's all we offer. Congregations must be more self-aware of how different people can feel excluded or not welcome. This counts for not just events but even conversations we have within the congregation and the church at large. So, singles, whatever your circumstances and present inclinations to remain so, you are welcome.

But I do not apologize for being pro-marriage. *In fact, I believe that should be our basic posture.* Let me put it this way . . . as someone who dated my now-wife for two years with no plan to marry, whose then-girlfriend (now wife) burst into tears when I mocked marriage, who then realized what she *really* wanted was to get married, who then asked her to marry,

---

6. Being "chaste" isn't the same as being "celibate" and being "celibate" doesn't always lead to "chastity." A single needs both. Put another way, celibacy fits into a life of chastity for a single person.

7. Direct feedback I have received from singles over the years.

8. 1 Cor 7:2 (my emphasis and transliteration).

but then who had too long of an engagement, and then who *intentionally* waited eight years after marriage before trying to start a family, as someone who has followed the script set out by the culture with respect to dating, marriage, and a bunch of other stuff . . . *let me say that I know the pitfalls and the rationales out there.* Again, I speak from my own experiences and from a place of having done some of these things poorly in the past.

SOCIAL EVENTS THAT ALLOW FOR MEN AND WOMEN TO MEET (THE NEW "OLD THING")

I recently was talking to a home-bound member who is ninety-one years old. She is one of thirteen children, further down in the birth order. I asked her about dating in her day and how it was that men and women found someone to marry. She said something very interesting.

> Basically, the boys of the neighborhood and the girls would get together around a social club or event. My brothers had a baseball team with other guys that lived around, and the girls would form a cheerleading group that went to the games. The two groups would interact and people would meet . . . and, well, then people would get married.

It sounds so simple, so innocent. Compared to how we do it, it probably was! I asked her how she met her husband of sixty-five plus years. "The Walther League," she replied. The Walther League was a German Lutheran social organization established in 1893, as a sort of answer to the YMCA. After World War I and the rapid transition of most congregations from German speaking to English, the Walther League was the locus of many interactions between young Lutheran men and women. Through a coordination of a wide range of events, including an annual convention, summer camps, choirs, and sporting events, people of marriageable age interacted and got married. While there were some issues with messaging,[9] the Walther League functioned for several generations as a place within the LCMS for young people to meet and marry.

While not advocating a repristination project by restoring the Walther League to its formerly flawed "glory," perhaps we might consider at the congregational (and multi-congregational) level a sort of social space

9. One illuminating quote showing the way the League's mission was affected by the culture is from Elmer Witt, the executive director: "God created sexuality and calls us to live fully and freely as sexual beings" (Witt, "Life Can Be Sexual," 7–8). Yikes.

where marriageable men and women could meet, mingle, and perhaps find a mate to marry. Is it so wrong to desire that our sons and daughters marry other Christian sons and daughters? Isn't it a noble thing to find an appropriate way for men and women to socialize, to interact, to talk in a fun group setting? I am not advocating more youth groups for teens or "singles" groups for older adults. Very often (though well-intentioned) these devolve into worldly social clubs disconnected from the worship life of the church. My own experience with youth groups was pretty poor and the chaperone situation was, let us say, far from ideal. I don't think that has changed much. Youth groups really belong to the realm of the family as teenage youths are still growing children! What I am advocating is that congregations *intentionally host events for people of marriageable age* that are fun, wholesome, and purposeful. The goal is to give young adults[10] a place and opportunity to meet someone from the opposite sex and get to know them. At the same time, these groups would be directly connected to the church's doctrine, practice, and worship. In other words, the people who would come to these social events would *already be part of the worship life of the congregation or neighboring congregations.* Not advocating "singles nights" open to the community! There are in fact congregations already doing what I suggest.[11] We certainly don't need another broad denominational program. We need a grassroots approach. We need congregational leadership to be thoughtful and intentional about how we go about encouraging marriage in a day and age where arranged marriage is not feasible. We need to help singles meet other singles who desire to marry. As a pastor of a smaller-sized parish, this project would have to be expanded to include other local congregations to cast the largest and most reasonable geographical net.

IN-HOUSE MATCHMAKERS (TURN THEM LOOSE!)

I got to know a young man who had recently become a member of a congregation I was serving. He was twenty-five, single, handsome, employed, out on his own, and interested in dating. A unicorn! Some elder ladies of

---

10. I envision both people who are still connected to their families and others who are now out on their own, maybe geographically distant from their family and home congregation.

11. There are two congregations in the St. Louis area that I know of—Village Lutheran in the St. Louis, Missouri, area has what is called Quarter Life events and St. Paul's in Hamel, Illinois, a reboot of the Walther League.

the congregation saw an opportunity to "help him out." They whispered together and came up with a matchmaking plan—fix him up with an eligible, lovely young lady who was also a member of the congregation, about the same age. Nudges were made—the two of them should perhaps get together for a cup of coffee or go for a walk? What about going together to the upcoming Sausage Supper? However, the young man found out about these women "interfering" in his business, sticking their noses in where they don't belong. *He was furious.* How dare they! The nerve! He would date whom he wanted, when he wanted, thank you. He vented to me one afternoon about how aggravated he was by the situation.

> "I cannot believe these women! Who do they think they are?"
> "They are trying to set you up on a date . . ."
> "It's none of their business! They should stay out of it!"
> "I just think they're trying to help . . ."
> "I don't need their help!"
> "Don't you want to meet girls?"
> "Of course. I'd rather do it on my own."
> "How's that working for you?"
> *Silence.*
> "Where do you propose to meet these girls?"
> "Where would you have me meet them?" (potential sarcasm)
> "I don't know . . . at church! Where else—a bar?" (full-on sarcasm)
> *More silence.*
> "Maybe you shouldn't be mad, but grateful."
> *Staring daggers.*

Nothing came of this. He wasn't receptive. And sometimes it doesn't work out. But my main point—there is a lot of pressure on young men and women to meet a mate to marry (those who truly want to). We should help them (see above). Besides, what's really wrong with matchmaking? Truth be told, I might not have been keen on it either. But what's the alternative? Besides, there are women I know who are really good at putting people together. They are gifted at picking out individual characteristics that are compatible, who have a sense of "fit," who know intuitively who might go with whom.[12] It's not that we need committees or a Board of Social Engagement. But what if we were a little more nosy, a little less defensive, and empowered ladies of the congregation to "do their thing"? What would it look like? I don't know . . . but maybe we could have a quiet word with a few of them and then stay out of their way!

12. It turns out that "women's intuition" is a real thing.

The alternative is to let young people fend for themselves. To quote, well, myself, "How's that working out?" Perhaps if more people tacitly acknowledged the need, and quietly inquired on behalf of eligible matches (with the consent of the "matchees" and families), we would encourage men and women to appropriately date and marry. And then have families of their own. We don't need to use apps or sites or leave people to their own devices. We need to tap into a resource already in place—*the people of God in a place who have our best interests in mind.* People who might know a thing or two about a thing or two.

FOR THE PASTORS (TO SERVE THEIR PEOPLE BETTER)

I address pastors specifically. We have the greatest responsibility in the congregation. We are the spiritual shepherds of our flock's bodies and souls. We are going to be held accountable to how faithfully we preached God's truth—all of it.[13] So, we need to start finding ways to preach against *PIL* from the pulpit routinely, *so that our flocks know clearly where we stand and what God says about it, especially pornography.* Let me be clear—the sermon is the moment of proclamation of the gospel. But the sermon can also serve as a way to engage in all of God's truth. We can no longer assume that everyone's on the same page. It might make for some uncomfortable moments. To be sure, we should be aware of little ears and innocent hearts. But to say *nothing* is not an option. Not anymore. If anything, it counts as tacit approval.

So, what might this look like? First of all, it means *not* steering away from preaching on a reading because it might be uncomfortable. It means *looking for opportunities* in the assigned readings to proclaim Law and Gospel on the topic of *PIL*. It doesn't mean that every sermon is about pornography . . . but some of them should be. Especially if the congregation hears a text from St. Paul condemning *porneia*. For instance, in the Three-Year Lectionary: Series B, on Epiphany 2, the epistle for that day is 1 Cor 6:12–20. Although referenced in part 2 above, I again provide a portion of it below (my emphasis).

> The body is not meant for sexual immorality, but for the Lord, and the Lord for the body. And God raised the Lord and will also raise us up by his power. Do you not know that your bodies are

13. "Not many of you should become teachers, my brothers, for you know that we who teach will be judged with greater strictness" (Jas 3:1).

> members of Christ? *Shall I then take the members of Christ and make them members of a prostitute*? Never! Or do you not know that he who is joined to a prostitute becomes one body with her? For, as it is written, "The two will become one flesh." But he who is joined to the Lord becomes one spirit with him. *Flee from sexual immorality*. Every other sin a person commits is outside the body, but the sexually immoral person sins against his own body. Or do you not know that your body is a temple of the Holy Spirit within you, whom you have from God? *You are not your own, for you were bought with a price. So glorify God in your body.*

This will be heard by all on Sunday morning. It's not a "moralistic" or a "works righteousness" text, but a portion of Paul's letter dealing with a *known climate in the body of Christ constantly confronted with* porneia. It has tremendous gospel handles that allow the preacher to proclaim the full-throated forgiveness of Jesus. But it also gives opportunity to discuss the sexual sins and temptations we all face in our present age. What if pastors looked for these texts in the lectionary and let the people hear what God's word has to say about pornography and *PIL*? What if we applied God's condemnation and promise to his people in a direct and meaningful way?

What if you are a "one-year" guy?[14] Galatians 5:16–24 comes up every year on Trinity 14. Again, I provide the text (my emphasis).

> But I say, walk by the Spirit, and you will not gratify the desires of the flesh. For the desires of the flesh are against the Spirit, and the desires of the Spirit are against the flesh, for these are opposed to each other, to keep you from doing the things you want to do. But if you are led by the Spirit, you are not under the law. Now the works of the flesh are evident: *sexual immorality*, impurity, sensuality, idolatry, sorcery, enmity, strife, jealousy, fits of anger, rivalries, dissensions, divisions, envy, drunkenness, orgies, and things like these. I warn you, as I warned you before, *that those who do such things will not inherit the kingdom of God*. But the fruit of the Spirit is love, joy, peace, patience, kindness, goodness, faithfulness, gentleness, self-control; against such things there is no law. *And those who belong to Christ Jesus have crucified the flesh with its passions and desires.*

---

14. For those of you unfamiliar, the lectionaries referenced are a three and one year cycle of readings, organized around what was historically read in the church at different times of the year.

This reading deals with a myriad of issues (including *porneia*) but also the role of the Holy Spirit in bearing fruit in the life of the believer. The preacher could talk about the tension we all feel of the Spirit's work *alone* in bearing fruit but the responsibility we have to "walk by the Spirit." All people relate to this tension. "We are to bear good fruit but we still keep sinning!" Exactly. "How should we consider this, Pastor? Receiving salvation by grace through faith in Christ, then what might we do?" The preacher can address *porneia* and still faithfully proclaim the gospel.

There are other ways for a pastor to engage the congregation. Conducting a Bible study series on letters of Paul, or cultural topics related to *PIL*. Leading chapel at local Christian high schools gives excellent opportunities to directly engage with a target audience on the topic of pornography. Newsletters, blog posts, town hall meetings, retreats are all appropriate forums. Pastors have a voice and maybe even a bit of influence. We just have to use it. But what we cannot do is stay silent and assume that people are fully aware and engaged. Or pretend that pornography isn't an issue in your church. *Our silence is tacit acceptance.* I speak from first-hand experience. To attend a church year in and year out and *never* hear anything about pornography leaves the impression that it doesn't matter or isn't a concern. And clearly, it is.

Chapter Fifteen

A Conversation on the Sixth (or Seventh) Commandment

ANOTHER TOPIC WE ARE reticent to mention is sex/human sexuality. This needs to be reclaimed by the church. The jab often made against so-called conservative[1] Christians by so-called progressives—*you're all a bunch of repressed sexual prudes*. "You hate sex!" Not true. God is the author of sex. Rightly ordered between a married man and woman, *sex is a good gift of God*. It is the physical and intimate way God binds together husband and wife. So, the problem is not sex. The problem is perversion—the twisting of what is good into something evil. But perversion does not *destroy* the good. A long-standing theological maxim in the church: *abusus non tollit, sed confirmat substantiam.*[2] That is, "Misuse does not destroy the substance, but confirms its existence." To quote Martin Luther, "Gold remains no less gold if a harlot wears it in sin and shame." Let's stop letting the devil, the world, and our sinful flesh run roughshod over what God has given and ordained. In other words, stop letting the culture define sexuality. Instead, let us turn to Christ for mercy, to the Spirit for regeneration and formation, and our Creator for order. In that spirit, we turn to Luther for much-needed guidance on rightly ordered human sexuality.

1. By "conservative," I truly mean those who want to conserve God's truth and standards.

2. Latin always sounds cooler.

One of the best places in all of Luther's writings for a conversation about sex are the Catechisms. The Small Catechism's explanation to the Sixth Commandment,[3] "You shall not commit adultery," is: "*We should fear and love God so that we lead a sexually pure and decent life in what we say and do, and husband and wife love and honor each other.*"[4] A straightforward exposition of Scripture and God's will. But does Luther say more? You bet. The Small Catechism is actually drawn from the Large. It is there that Luther grounds the Sixth Commandment's purpose in the "second table of the law"—*to guard against harming our neighbor in any way.* The second table starts with the walk of father and mother in the Fourth, then God's desire to "remove the root and source that embitters our heart toward our neighbor"[5] in the Fifth. The Sixth then proceeds to speak of one's nearest neighbor—the spouse. Luther vividly sets the cultural context.

> But inasmuch as there is such a shameless mess and cesspool of all sorts of immorality and indecency among us, this commandment is also directed against every form of unchastity, no matter what it is called. Not only is the outward act forbidden, but also every kind of cause, provocation, and means, so that your heart, your lips, and your entire body may be chaste and afford no occasion, aid, or encouragement to unchastity.[6]

It's almost as if Luther could see into our own situation! Of course, the problem of *PIL* has been manifested in every epoch of time. But the Sixth Commandment speaks broadly to the topic we are discussing, for not only is adultery forbidden, "but also every kind of cause, provocation, and means, so that your heart, your lips, and your entire body may be chaste and afford no occasion, aid, or encouragement to unchastity."[7] The commandment *speaks to the entire person and way of life* while surrounded by every by every manner of perversion. While marriage and one's spouse is the chief target, the neighbor is always in view.

> Not only that, but you are to defend, protect, and rescue your neighbors whenever they are in danger or need, and, moreover, even aid and assist them so that they may retain their honor.

---

3. In the Roman Catholic and Lutheran tradition this is the Sixth commandment, but for many Protestants, it is numbered as the Seventh.

4. Luther, *Luther's Small Catechism*, 14.

5. Kolb and Wengert, *Book of Concord*, 411.

6. Kolb and Wengert, *Book of Concord*, 414.

7. Kolb and Wengert, *Book of Concord*, 414.

> Whenever you fail to do this (although you could prevent a wrong)
> or do not even lift a finger (as if it were none of your business), *you
> are just as guilty as the culprit who commits the act.*[8] In short, all
> are required both to live chastely themselves and also to help their
> neighbors to do the same.[9]

Luther makes two claims to marriage's importance. First, Luther emphasizes "how highly God honors and praises this walk of life, endorsing and
protecting it by his commandment."[10] Such a simple statement, but one
many (even in the church) have forgotten. We treat marriage as a personal
choice, a lifestyle, something that may be done or not. But Luther puts it on
the highest of planes, not only commending it, but putting it *above every
other station of life.*

> [God] endorsed [marriage] above in the Fourth Commandment,
> "You shall honor father and mother." But here, as I said, he has
> secured and protected it. For the following reasons he also wishes
> us to honor, maintain, and cherish it as a divine and blessed walk
> of life. He has established it *before all others as the first of all institu-
> tions,* and he created man and woman differently (as is evident)
> not for indecency but to be true to each other, to be fruitful, to
> beget children, and to nurture and bring them up to the glory of
> God. God has therefore blessed this walk of life most richly, above
> all others, and, in addition, has supplied and endowed it with ev-
> erything in the world in order that this walk of life might be richly
> provided for. Married life is no matter for jest or idle curiosity, but
> it is a glorious institution and an object of God's serious concern.
> For it is of utmost importance to him that persons be brought up
> to serve the world, to promote knowledge of God, godly living,
> and all virtues, and to fight against wickedness and the devil.[11]

What is your reaction to this? I have to admit, the first time I seriously
considered Luther's very simple argumentation, I was taken aback at how
strongly he endorsed something that for most of my young life I considered
as something people did as it suited them. But here, "this glorious institution" is praised beyond any other calling. Do contemporary Christians
broadly share this view? Perhaps in theory, but in practice, there is a lot
to be desired. But it's the second claim Luther makes that ties marriage

8. My emphasis. Hereafter in this chapter, italics used in the quotes are my emphasis.

9. Kolb and Wengert, *Book of Concord*, 414.

10. Kolb and Wengert, *Book of Concord*, 414.

11. Kolb and Wengert, *Book of Concord*, 414.

directly into our discussion of *PIL*. Luther argues that marriage is a necessary walk of life to keep immorality and unchastity in check.

> In the second place, you should also remember that it is not just an honorable walk of life but also *a necessary one*; it is solemnly *commanded by God that in general both men and women of all walks of life, who have been created for it, shall be found in this walk of life.* To be sure, there are some (albeit rare) exceptions whom God has especially exempted, in that some are unsuited for married life, or others God has released by a high, supernatural gift so that they can maintain chastity outside of marriage. Where nature functions as God implanted it, *however, it is not possible to remain chaste outside of marriage*; for flesh and blood remain flesh and blood, and natural inclinations and stimulations proceed *unrestrained and unimpeded,* as everyone observes and experiences. Therefore, to make it easier for people to avoid unchastity in some measure, God has established marriage, so that all may have their allotted portion and be satisfied with it—although here, too, God's grace is still required to keep the heart pure.[12]

Luther's common sense statements astound, because *we never talk this way about marriage.* We live in an era of delayed marriage, of making it optional or not for everyone, something done "when the time is right." But Luther sees it as a necessity, *that people might not burn in unchastity and lust and look for other outlets.* He knows (from personal experience no doubt!) that men and women will turn to other places for "relief." This is a direct connection to the problem of pornography and the topic of marriage—for if people are used to "taking care of their own needs" the question becomes, "What do I need marriage for? I have myself!"[13] This is the way many young men view marriage, seeing fornication and pornography as a replacement.

Luther's context is important to consider. He is writing to people *exiting* the Roman Papal Era (what he calls the "papal crowd") and monasticism. People would put away their daughters to take vows of perpetual chastity in order to gain holiness. Men would take vows of chastity as part of their holy orders. Luther had done this himself. But he knew that this was not only against God's command and institution, *but that it was unnatural.* For many people who took such vows ended up committing gross and carnal sins.

---

12. Kolb and Wengert, *Book of Concord*, 414–15.
13. Sadly, I have heard this expressed by more than one male in my life.

> For no one has so little love and inclination for chastity as those who under the guise of great sanctity avoid marriage and either indulge in open and shameless fornication or secretly do even worse—things too evil to mention, as unfortunately has been experienced all too often. In short, even though they abstain from the act, yet their hearts remain so full of unchaste thoughts and evil desires that they suffer incessant ragings of secret passion, which can be avoided in married life.[14]

Even from a different era, a strong warning is given as to what would happen if marriage was discouraged or treated with indifference. Unchaste thoughts, evil desires, and ragings of secret passion run amok in a "marriage-less" society.[15] But Luther's aim is to encourage. He is using the Sixth Commandment to catechize his people and applying it to the practical aspect of the faith. He is encouraging marriage and the praise and honor it bestows, but also the necessity of what it curbs. This is the work of God's Law—to curb, to accuse, and to bless the Christian.

> I say these things in order that our young people may be led to acquire a desire for married life and know that it is a blessed and God-pleasing walk of life. Thus it may in due time regain its proper honor, and there may be less of the filthy, dissolute, disorderly conduct that is now so rampant everywhere in public prostitution and other shameful vices resulting from contempt of married life. Therefore parents and governmental authorities have the duty of so supervising the youth that they will be brought up with decency and respectability and, when they are grown, will be married honorably in the fear of God. Then God would add his blessing and grace so that they might have joy and happiness in their married life.[16]

To connect it directly to our topic, *God gives marriage to his creation primarily for procreation, but also that his creatures may avoid* porneia *and a licentious lifestyle by serving only themselves and their own prurient interests.* Certainly, growing up in my Lutheran parochial school, in youth groups (both Lutheran and non-Lutheran), I never heard marriage spoken of in this way. Never. In some corners, the tide has turned a bit. But I suspect that many young adults are mostly left to make their own choices with little

14. Kolb and Wengert, *Book of Concord*, 415.

15. This doesn't even take into account the issue of the plummeting birthrate in our country, which has been below replacement level for nearly a decade.

16. Kolb and Wengert, *Book of Concord*, 415.

or no guidance from their parents and the church. What if we were to take Luther, and more importantly, God's word and will seriously?

Perhaps we might raise our sons and daughters with an eye to marriage and parenthood. Perhaps we talk of these things as not only options but as *goals for life*. Perhaps we train them in biological, created roles and how these are lived out in marriage. While not condemning singles, we also recognize that chaste self-control is not given to most people. We see that modeling marriage, prizing it as a gift of God, might even redirect people from finding pleasure outside of the marriage bed. That marriage is the place for God-ordained beautiful intimacy between a husband and wife. That sex is not separated from pleasure (the trope so often slung at people like me) but to be enjoyed in the right sphere within God's order and design. What might happen in our congregations, and even our own communities, if we incorporated these views?

Let's let Luther have the final say.

> Let it be said in conclusion that this commandment requires *all people not only to live chastely in deed, word, and thought in their particular situation* (that is, especially in marriage as a walk of life), but also to love and cherish the spouse whom God has given them. Wherever marital chastity is to be maintained, above all it is essential that husband and wife live together in love and harmony, cherishing each other wholeheartedly and with perfect fidelity. This is one of the chief ways to make chastity attractive and desirable. *Under such conditions chastity always follows spontaneously without any command.* This is why St. Paul so urgently admonishes married couples to love and honor each other. Here again you have a precious good work—indeed, many great works—in which you can happily boast over against all "spiritual walks of life" that are chosen without God's Word and commandment.[17]

17. Kolb and Wengert, *Book of Concord*, 415–16.

Chapter Sixteen

Being a "Holy Hypocrite"

Thus, when you give to the needy, sound no trumpet before you, as *the hypocrites* do in the synagogues and in the streets, that they may be praised by others. Truly, I say to you, they have received their reward . . . And when you pray, *you must not be like the hypocrites.* For they love to stand and pray in the synagogues and at the street corners, that they may be seen by others. Truly, I say to you, they have received their reward . . . And when you fast, do not look gloomy *like the hypocrites,* for they disfigure their faces that their fasting may be seen by others. Truly, I say to you, they have received their reward.

—Matt 6:2, 5, 16

Hypocrites are bad, right? We don't want to be a hypocrite! Of all the things that Christians get called (even by other Christians), the one invective that stings most is *judgmental hypocrite.* And they seem to have Jesus to back them up! For Jesus says hypocrites are self-serving, self-righteous, and sanctimonious (self-holy). We don't want to be a hypocrite, but it seems that no matter what we do, we are equated with them. "But I thought the title of this section is 'Being a Hypocrite'? Doesn't that go against what Jesus says?" Well, umm . . . yes? No? Kinda?

I get to what I mean in a moment. But to start, let's be clear with our terms and definitions. What is a hypocrite in Jesus' context? Hypocrisy is a *jarring contradiction between outward appearance and inward lack of righteousness.* A hypocrite is someone who says one thing but does another. Or does one thing while saying another. Consider Matt 7:3–5.

> Why do you see the speck that is in your brother's eye, but do not notice the log that is in your own eye? Or how can you say to your brother, "Let me take the speck out of your eye," when there is the log in your own eye? You hypocrite, first take the log out of your own eye, and then you will see clearly to take the speck out of your brother's eye.

Jesus condemns those who judge others for their wrongdoing *but fail to see their own sin.* Any sinner, Jesus says, is to deal with one's own sin first before denouncing another. The hypocrite is one who fails to do God's will, but hides behind the pious appearance of outward conduct. So, the root cause of hypocrisy is sin and failure to address it.

A LIFE OF REPENTANCE AND FORGIVENESS

Note that in statements about hypocrisy and hypocrites, *Jesus never condones sinful behavior of any kind.* And he does not say *not* to denounce sin. What he actually says is, "Judge not, that you be not judged. For with the judgment you pronounce you will be judged, and with the measure you use it will be measured to you."[1] Whatever standard one uses, the same standard is used against the one judging. By the way, that standard is God's Law! So, dealing with "hypocrisy" is first to deal with one's own sin. "For there is no distinction: for all have sinned and fall short of the glory of God."[2] Fall short is a bit bland—more like to *completely lack something due to one's fault or failure.* We are all sinners, through and through. No one is exempt. No one achieves righteousness on own's one. So, what is a sinful person to do? Run to the cross and receive the forgiveness of Jesus. The next part of Paul's verse in Romans 3: *"and are justified by his grace as a gift, through the redemption that is in Christ Jesus, whom God put forward as a propitiation by his blood, to be received by faith."* We are put in right standing with God through the redemptive work of Jesus. Jesus is the one whose

1. Matt 7:1–2.
2. Rom 3:23.

blood covers every sin; there is only one source of forgiveness. We receive this as a gift—God's unmerited favor given to us. We don't earn it or buy it. We just receive. While this forgiveness is achieved through the one-time act of Jesus on the cross, we need to hear the word of forgiveness again and again. Because we continue to "daily sin much and indeed deserve nothing but punishment."[3] So, we are to be repentant of our own sin. We are to be aware of it, sorry for it, and own it. But that's half of it. We are also to trust in the forgiveness Jesus gives, that it does what it says—absolves us from guilt and allows us to live in the mercy of God.[4]

Experientially, the forgiveness given is *that which is heard*. It is spoken by another. It is spoken by the pastor, both publicly and privately, in worship and private confession. It is delivered in the Supper, but again spoken in the words "Given and shed for you." The *for you* is the chief thing in the Sacrament, for it is forgiveness.[5] Forgiveness is also shared by the saints to the saints. While we are sinners, we are also saints—declared holy ones by Jesus through the Spirit. So, in the priesthood of all believers,[6] we do the work of absolution by declaring forgiveness to one another. This forgiveness of Jesus is heard in the life of worship, in the life of faith, in the life of body of Christ.

CALLING SIN A SIN WITH BOLDNESS AND CLARITY

So, in the forgiveness of Jesus, standing justified before the Father by the blood of Jesus, we then can boldly call anything contrary to the will of God what it is—*sin*. When non- or nominal Christians[7] are quick to call us hypocrites, it is usually done in defense of some sort of wicked behavior. Let me try to explain the logic. Person A tells Person B that they have sinned. Person B calls Person A a "hypocrite," indicating that Person A has done just as many sinful things as Person B. Person A therefore, has no right to judge Person B because they are just as big a sinner. Person B might even bring up the aforementioned words of Jesus to support their

3. *Luther's Small Catechism*, "The Lord's Prayer, Explanation to the Fifth Petition," 21.

4. Repentance is both contrition for sin and faith in the promise of forgiveness.

5. Kolb and Wengert, *Book of Concord*, 469.

6. 1 Pet 2:9–10.

7. I use this term not as an insult, but to refer to those who claim to be Christian but want nothing to do with Jesus. In other words, they are Christian *in name only*.

own condemnation of hypocrisy.[8] Person A cowers and slinks away, having been called a hypocrite. And the sin that was addressed is left to fester and grow. This is in part where we have lost the cultural battle on issues like homosexuality, pornography, co-habitation, and a whole host of others. *We never get past the "hypocrisy" charge in the public square.*

Calling sin a sin is not "being judgmental." *Calling sin a sin is what the body of Christ is supposed to do.* Living in the mercy of God, we are to condemn sinful behavior in our own lives, in the lives of our families, in the lives (gasp!) of our neighbors, and even in the lives of our community and government. And if you think I'm "being judgmental," then read the Bible! Listen to Jesus. Listen to Paul. But we are called to be holy ones that we might remove sin from our midst and deal with it in the plain light of day. Especially in the church. If you recall our earlier discussion of 1 Cor 5:9–13, Paul is dealing with those "inside the church." The goal of condemnation, though, is not to go on a sanctimonious power trip, but the goal is always *repentance.* Turn from sin and turn back to Jesus. This gets messy, and it's hard and uncomfortable, but we are *called to belong to Jesus Christ*[9] and *called to be saints.*[10] So, when we see sin in our lives and practiced in our midst, we are to condemn it. How we go about this is another conversation (we are to speak the truth in love),[11] but my purpose here is to talk about *being a holy hypocrite* that we might full-throatedly condemn *PIL.* What might this look like?

THE WOMAN AND THE SON

To be called a hypocrite often stops people from doing their duties in their given vocations. Not just from the sting of the charge, but because of their own guilt. They feel crippled because of their past. They feel like they can't say anything because at one time they were doing the same things. There are people who might read this book, who knew me in a former time, and will tell anyone who will listen how big of a hypocrite I am. It is a powerful hindrance, even within the church, to living out a repentant and faithful life. However, whatever our pasts, whatever mistakes we've made, we must

---

8. It's amazing the Bible scholarship on display in these conversations!

9. Rom 1:6.

10. Rom 1:7.

11. Passive-aggressively posting something on Facebook is not the answer!

be willing to be "holy hypocrites." The best way to unpack this is through the following scenario:

> While in high school and during college, a certain woman lived a licentious lifestyle. She engaged in sexual immorality, drunkenness, and co-habitation. Since that time, she became more regular in her worship habits, was mentored by other Christian women, and *she repented of her past sins*. She even confessed them privately to her pastor and received absolution for those things that deeply troubled her heart. She changed her life, all in the name of Jesus and by the power of the Holy Spirit. This woman eventually met a man, got married, and raised a family in the faith as best they could.
>
> One of the woman's sons has now gone off to college. During this time, he has fallen in with "a crowd." He has begun to drink excessively and have sexual relationships with several girls. While his mother doesn't know the details, she knows enough. She's lived the life and knows the signs. She's tried talking with him about his behavior, but is largely ignored. She finds out that her son is now living with a girl. She knows nothing about her. He has hidden this from her, but again, a mother knows. Besides, she knows lying when she sees it! She wants to confront her son. He clearly is living against God's will. He's stopped attending worship, and no longer comes around his parents.
>
> The underlying issue she faces is tremendous guilt. She feels like a hypocrite, because when she was his age, *she did the very same things*. How can she say anything to him now? How can she "judge" his lifestyle? Besides, while her son doesn't know details, he has learned about some of *her* past. He's even made comments about "not judging him" considering the things that she did! However, this feeling of being a hypocrite is very strong. She doesn't feel like she has a leg to stand on. But she also knows that her son's immoral life is not God pleasing. She is worried about his standing before God; has he walked away from the faith? Has he rejected Jesus?
>
> The woman, in desperation, comes to talk to her pastor. She shares these things with him (in perfect confidence) and asks his counsel. He (re)assures her that she is a child of God and forgiven of her past by the blood of Jesus.[12] While she knows this (she came to terms with her past long ago), it is comforting to once more hear the words of forgiveness. But the conflict remains: *who is she to say anything to her son?*

---

12. It is worth noting how Satan will continue to bring up our past up again and again to drive us to despair.

This is where the pastor has to say: "*Be a hypocrite.*" It is her duty to lovingly[13] tell her son that he is sinning and endangering his faith. While the promises God makes are certain and sure, people can and do walk away of their own, free, sinful will. But she must be a holy hypocrite—*saying and exhorting one thing when she (perhaps) has lived and done another.* She must be willing to say to her son: what you're doing is wrong, sinful, and goes against God's Law. She knows first-hand how destructive this lifestyle can be, and she must confront her son in his sinful behavior.

There is a marked difference in what Jesus speaks of and what this woman is going through. *The difference is in repentance and forgiveness.* The woman has clearly seen the beam in her own eye, and it has been removed by Jesus! She is free from that log. She can see clearly now. She is still a sinner, till the day she dies, but she is also a forgiven saint. She has been made holy by the Spirit. He is working in her life, leading and guiding her, and bringing her back to Jesus. This is what is called *sanctification*—a fancy word for the Spirit's work.[14] And, as the pastor tells her, the goal in confronting her son is that he would be led to repentance, just like she was, and that he would change his life.

BEING A HOLY HYPOCRITE

In every other area of life, we have no problem telling our children and grandchildren of our past experiences in an effort to caution them to not make the mistakes we made. We have no compunction about warning our kids not to use credit cards if we've had bankruptcy in our past, or not to drop out of college if we have regrets over an unfinished degree. But with matters of the faith and morality, we are scared to death of being called a hypocrite, of feeling like one, and looking like one in the eyes of the world. In response to this fear, I say, *be a holy hypocrite.* Be bold in saying, "I don't want you to do the same, stupid, wicked, evil things that I did! Please don't do it! It's wrong! God condemns it. Please repent of your sin and return to Jesus." *That should be our stance.* No, we don't say one thing while doing another. We don't live a corrupt lifestyle while preaching piety. We don't watch porn secretly while publicly condemning sexual sin. Our inner life and outer life should match. And when it doesn't, we repent and, in the forgiveness

13. Love does not equal being nice or ignoring sin.

14. The work of sanctification is ongoing in the life of the Christian. As long as we live in the "old age," we need the Spirit's work of making us holy.

of Jesus, do better. God will give us the power and strength to change. I have seen it firsthand. But we owe it to our families and congregations to confront lies, immorality, and perversion where we see it. Because when we don't, we lose. Our families lose. Our congregations lose. Our society comes apart at the seams. What we need is more "holy hypocrites"—*people who are willing to do and say something different than what they've said and done in the past*. We must pass this life of faith we've been given down to the next generation. Part of that is teaching the faith, but another is confronting sin where it lies and directing hearts and minds to Christ.

Chapter Seventeen

Mentioning the Unmentionables
Going Forward

THIS ENTIRE ENTERPRISE OF diagnosing, critiquing, and offering a course of action for the individual, the family, and the church with respect to pornography and related topics is an ambitious task. But it's necessary. We've been silent too long on things we should have been teaching and admonishing, while at times talking about every other gross subject with frankness. So, I *mention the unmentionables* but with a goal—that you are convicted for your part in the silence and are spurred to start talking about the topic of pornography and *PIL*. Your voice matters! I know I'm convicted for my silence. It's what led to this whole project! Everyone has something to do, a part to play, a dog in the fight. Even if you are done with raising kids, or never had a family, *we are all called to live lives of holiness until the day the Lord calls us home.* We don't put our purity project before the work of Christ (we're not legalists!), but we don't ignore piety because we are afraid of becoming too "works righteous." In my humble opinion, being preoccupied with piety and works have not been the church's problem in my lifetime!

"CALLING A THING WHAT IT IS"

As I draw to a close, I invoke Martin Luther a final time. While Lutheran theology pervades this entire piece, chapter 16 is the only explicitly

"Lutheran" part of the book. But running like a thread through everything is a shorthand Lutheran phrase that sets the tone: *calling a thing what it is.* So, where does this come from, and what did it mean for Luther? What does it mean for us? The phrase is derived from one of Luther's earliest works, *The Heidelberg Disputation.* In the spring of 1518, Luther left Wittenberg to attend the general convocation of the German Augustinians in Heidelberg on April 25. Luther had posted his 95 Theses the prior year for debate, but no one took him up on the disputation he desired. Instead, there were many who wanted to silence him or extract an apology. The vicar of Luther's order, Johann Staupitz, to avoid further controversy, asked him to prepare disputations, not on the 95 Theses, but concerning sin, free will, and grace.[1] Luther complied. He prepared twenty-eight theological and twelve philosophical theses (along with their proofs) for debate. It is the proof to the twenty-first theological thesis relevant for our discussion.

> A theologian of glory calls evil good and good evil. A theologian of the cross *calls the thing what it actually is.*
> This is clear: He who does not know Christ does not know God hidden in suffering. Therefore he prefers works to suffering, glory to the cross, strength to weakness, wisdom to folly, and, in general, good to evil. These are the people whom the apostle calls "enemies of the cross of Christ" [Phil 3:18], for they hate the cross and suffering and love works and the glory of works. *Thus they call the good of the cross evil and the evil of a deed good.* God can be found only in suffering and the cross, as has already been said. Therefore the friends of the cross say that the cross is good and works are evil, for through the cross works are destroyed and the old Adam, who is especially edified by works, is crucified. It is impossible for a person not to be puffed up by his good works unless he has first been deflated and destroyed by suffering and evil until he knows that he is worthless and that his works are not his but God's.[2]

As seen above, the God hidden in suffering, the Christ of the cross is the place where "works" are destroyed and the Old Adam is crucified. *Calling the good thing of the cross good is what a theologian of the cross does.* The cruciform theologian does not call "evil good and good evil." He cannot. While Luther was addressing a different context, one which held that works contributed to one's standing before God (works righteousness), he hits on an idea truly important for us. We are not to deal in opposites. We are not

---

1. These were common theological topics of the day.
2. Luther, *Luther's Works,* 31:53 (my emphasis).

to traffic in perverse things and call them good or even let them pass as acceptable. *We are to call a thing what it is.* By mentioning the unmentionable things—calling out *PIL* in our lives and condemning the ways we succumb to it—we are submitting ourselves to the reality of the cross. The cross destroys the works of evil. It condemns the self-satisfied sinner. "But God chose what is foolish in the world to shame the wise; God chose what is weak in the world to shame the strong."[3]

This is why we must show courage in the coming months and years. We must say what a thing is. We must call it out. We can do so winsomely, we can do so respectfully, we can do so in love. *But we must call it out.* This starts with our own lives. It starts with a fearless inventory of every "bad" thing we whitewash, and then with condemning it. Call it what it is. A sin is a sin is a sin. This is called repentance. Once we become like the rabble of Sodom, we are lost. So, showing courage, we say, "This behavior, this movie, this sentiment, this crass joke, this living situation . . ." is evil. It is wicked. It starts with you. Every single day. Confess your sin and turn to Christ for forgiveness.

But we don't do this for a heightened morality, climbing the ladder to God. Our works apart from Christ are rubbish. This book isn't about setting up a new way to receive God's favor. It is a call to the old way, the only way to redemption—through the suffering Savior who killed every single sin on the cross, who nailed every transgression to the tree, whose shed blood cleanses every single act of *PIL*. *What we are to do is to live as a theologian of the cross.* Returning to Jesus, again and again in repentance and faith. And in his mercy, we are to call good, good and evil, evil. We start this today, and every day going forward.

WHERE YOU FIND YOURSELF RIGHT NOW

Maybe you've read this book because you are struggling with pornography. Maybe out of curiosity. Maybe you've had a suspicion that things were bad, but hadn't connected the dots. Maybe you are looking for validation. Wherever you find yourself—father, mother, single, son, daughter, pastor, layperson—we all are sinners and are in need of the mercy of Christ. It is in that mercy, on the basis of that forgiveness, *that we can do better.* We must do better. There are things that are hard to change, hard to talk about. But let's begin the conversation. Let's start mentioning the unmentionables—*the*

3. 1 Cor 1:27.

things that for too long have stayed off our radar. To talk about them, to have the conversation, leads us to questions and then to faithful answers. The world of *porneia,* immorality and *licentiousness* isn't going away. But they feed on our silence. Let us shed some light and offer a Christian response, in the name of Jesus. Though we strain forward to what lies ahead, while we are here, we have responsibilities to our families and obligations to our communities. People who depend on us to do the right thing. So, we mention them *for them,* for their sake. To be stewards of what God has given us—our bodies, our families, our congregations.

So, in that Spirit, we are to call out things that have been unmentioned. Routinely ignored. If you are struggling with a pornography addiction, you must confess it, and seek help and reformation. Pastors, if we have a "co-habitating" couple in our congregation, we need to say something. Appropriately, pastorally. Parents, if your daughter is dressed inappropriately, you must say something. If your child is watching something they shouldn't, we exercise discipline. Christian brother or sister, if your friend is watching pornography, we encourage them to stop and seek assistance. We are to join our voices together and say, "Pornography is wicked. It has no place in our life." *We are not to ignore it anymore.*

At the same time, we don't have to say everything. This book intentionally leaves out details. We need not titillate. We need not say too much to cause offense, or "keep it real." We must use sanctified restraint, decorum, and modesty. We mention the offense without mentioning every single aspect. There is a tension in this, but it is our calling as ones who "walk by the Spirit." Let us keep in step with the Spirit by calling sin a sin but not letting our description undermine our proclamation. It might seem to be a fine line. But we need it . . . and our families and congregations need us now more than ever. They need our boldness and they need our discretion. They need our clarity and our restraint to not be crass. I leave you with this: "Be strong and courageous. Do not be frightened, and do not be dismayed, for the Lord your God is with you wherever you go."[4]

4. Josh 1:9b.

Sources, Resources, and Bibliography

Alter, Adam. *Irresistible: The Rise of the Addictive Technology and the Business of Keeping Us Hooked*. New York: Penguin, 2018.

Biermann, Joel D. *A Case for Character: Towards a Lutheran Virtue Ethics*. Minneapolis: Fortress, 2014.

Black, Sam. *The Porn Circuit: Understand Your Brain and Break Your Porn Habit in 90 Days*. Owosso, MI: Covenant Eyes, 2021.

Carr, Nicholas. *The Shallows: What the Internet Is Doing to Our Brains*. New York: Norton, 2020.

Cox, Daniel, et al. "How Prevalent Is Pornography?" Institute for Family Studies, May 2, 2022. https://ifstudies.org/blog/how-prevalent-is-pornography.

Curtis, Rebekah, and Rose Adle. *Lady Like: Living Biblically*. St. Louis: Concordia, 2015.

Esolen, Anthony. *No Apologies: Why Civilization Depends on the Strength of Men*. Washington, DC: Regnery, 2022.

———. *Out of the Ashes: Rebuilding American Culture*. Washington, DC: Regnery, 2017.

———. *Ten Ways to Destroy the Imagination of Your Child*. Wilmington, DE: Intercollegiate Studies Institute, 2010.

Fradd, Matt. *The Porn Myth: Exposing the Reality behind the Fantasy of Pornography*. San Francisco: Ignatius, 2017.

Gilkerson, Luke. "Survey of Christian Counselors about Pornography. CovenantEyes, Jul 30, 2021. https://www.covenanteyes.com/2008/12/18/survey-of-christian-counselors-about-pornography/.

Grudem, Wayne, ed. *Biblical Foundations for Manhood and Womanhood*. Wheaton, IL: Crossway, 2002.

Hemmer, Jeffrey. *Man Up! The Quest for Masculinity*. St. Louis: Concordia, 2017.

Kingdom Works Studios. "15 Mind-Blowing Statistics about Pornography and the Church." Mission Frontiers, Nov 1, 2020. https://www.missionfrontiers.org/issue/article/15-mind-blowing-statistics-about-pornography-and-the-church.

Kolb, Robert, and Timothy J. Wengert, eds. *The Book of Concord: The Confessions of the Evangelical Lutheran Church*. Minneapolis: Fortress, 2000.

Lawler, Leila Marie. "Emergency Summer Reading: The Gift of Modesty." Like Mother, Like Daughter Blog, Jul 30, 2022. http://likemotherlikedaughter.org/2022/07/emergency-summer-reading-the-gift-of-modesty/.

—————. *The Summa Domestica: Order and Wonder in Family Life.* 3 vols. Manchester, NH: Sophia Institute, 2021.

Luther, Martin. *Luther's Works.* Vol. 31, *Career of the Reformer I.* Minneapolis: Fortress, 1957.

—————. *Luther's Small Catechism.* St. Louis: Concordia, 2017.

Middendorf, Michael P. *Romans 1–8: The Concordia Commentary Series.* St. Louis: Concordia, 2013.

Pieper, Josef. *The Four Cardinal Virtues.* Notre Dame, IN: University of Notre Dame, 1966.

Raabe, Paul R., and James W. Voelz. "Why Exhort a Good Tree? Exhortation and Paraenesis in Romans." *Concordia Journal* 22.2 (1996) 154–63.

Rueger, Matthew. *Sexual Morality in a Christless World.* St. Louis: Concordia, 2016.

Safronova, Valeriya. "A Private-School Sex Educator Defends Her Methods." *New York Times*, Jul 2021. https://www.nytimes.com/2021/07/07/style/sex-educator-methods-defense.html.

Shalit, Wendy. *A Return to Modesty: Discovering the Lost Virtue.* New York: Simon & Schuster, 1999.

Smith, James K. A. *You Are What You Love: The Spiritual Power of Habit.* Grand Rapids: Baker, 2016.

Smith, Ralph A. "What Jeffrey Epstein Got Right." *Theopolis.* Aug 14, 2019. https://theopolisinstitute.com/leithart_post/what-jeffrey-epstein-got-right/.

Steinmann, Andrew E. *Proverbs.* Concordia Commentary Series. St. Louis: Concordia, 2009.

Stuckey, Allie Beth, and Ron Simmons. "Allie's Dad on the Economy, Fatherhood, and Raising Christians Kids." *Relatable with Allie Beth Stuckey*, episode 631, Jun 16, 2022. YouTube video. https://www.youtube.com/watch?v=Msis83spKxg.

Thistleton, Anthony C. *The First Epistle to the Corinthians.* New International Greek Testament Commentary Series. Grand Rapids: Eerdmans, 2000.

Venker, Suzanne. "Why the Feminist Life Script Makes Most Women Miserable: Joy Pullmann." *The Suzanne Venker Show*, Aug 17, 2019. Podcast.

Webroot. "Internet Pornography by the Numbers; A Significant Threat to Society." Accessed October 4, 2022. https://www.webroot.com/us/en/resources/tips-articles/internet-pornography-by-the-numbers.

Wikipedia. "Leggings." Accessed August 27, 2022. https://en.wikipedia.org/wiki/Leggings.

Winger, Thomas M. *Ephesians: The Concordia Commentary Series.* St. Louis: Concordia, 2015.

Witt, Elmer. "Life Can Be Sexual–Now." *Arena One* (June 1967) 7–8.